Computer Images

TIME® LIFE BOOKS

Other Publications:
THE ENCHANTED WORLD
YOUR HOME
THE KODAK LIBRARY OF CREATIVE PHOTOGRAPHY
GREAT MEALS IN MINUTES
THE CIVIL WAR
PLANET EARTH
COLLECTOR'S LIBRARY OF THE CIVIL WAR
THE EPIC OF FLIGHT
THE GOOD COOK
THE SEAFARERS
WORLD WAR II
HOME REPAIR AND IMPROVEMENT
THE OLD WEST

This volume is one of a series that examines various aspects of computer technology and the role computers play in modern life.

COVER

Interlinked toroidal, or doughnut-like, shapes and a cut-apart surface that unwraps from one toroid onto the other represent, in effect, a three-dimensional image of a sphere in four-dimensional space—an image virtually impossible for humans to visualize before the advent of the computer.

UNDERSTANDING COMPUTERS

Computer Images

BY THE EDITORS OF TIME-LIFE BOOKS
TIME-LIFE BOOKS, ALEXANDRIA, VIRGINIA

Contents

Discovering the Computer's Graphic Potential

A two-lane highway curves out of sight behind a sharp-edged outcropping of rock. In the hazy distance, a glimpse of ocean framed by California hills forms the backdrop for a double rainbow, produced like the reflecting pools in the road by a passing shower. It is difficult to accept that a scene as lyrical as *Road to Point Reyes (left)* is the embodiment of millions of binary integers, an elaborate paint-by-number work of art founded on the ones and zeros that are, in the end, the only language a computer can understand. Yet by harnessing the power of computers to the making of images, computer graphics exert almost as much influence in the world as the machines themselves. From industry to medicine, from engineering to entertainment, few fields remain untouched by this technology.

Computer graphics bring dead numbers to life. On the simplest level, the almost overwhelming amount of information generated in the course of running a company can be displayed graphically and thus interpreted and assimilated much more quickly. For example, a store owner might spend fruitless days poring over year-end totals and inventory results in computerized ledger sheets to determine which products he should stock to maximize profits. With the same information displayed as bar graphs and pie charts, solutions formerly obscured by the almost impenetrable jungle of figures immediately become obvious.

Computer imagery reveals the invisible. With the help of computer graphics, NMR and PET scanners *(pages 46-47)* let doctors look inside the body to diagnose diseases with a degree of confidence never before possible. A geologist used to reading the squiggles of a seismograph in response to exploratory underground explosions can view the same information on a computer screen as a cross-sectional image revealing subterranean features that may yield oil or minerals.

Computer graphics encourage trial and error; mistakes made on the computer cost little in money and lives compared with the potential costs of real experi-

Almost as realistic as a photograph, *Road to Point Reyes* is a computer-generated image produced by a team of computer graphics specialists. More than a dozen programs were required to create the image: The rocks, road, lake, hills, fence, rainbows, grass, flowering plants, sky, haze and even the ripples on the puddles were rendered by separate programs.

ments. For example, a computer model of an automobile may have been "driven" into a computer model of a brick wall so that engineers could observe the effect of the crash on computer-model passengers and improve the car's design. Other simulations are unabashedly entertaining. Film makers tap the talents of computer graphics wizards to create spaceships and other special effects that rival and sometimes surpass the work of model builders and background painters, Hollywood's traditional craftsmen of movie artifice.

These diverse applications of computer graphics all depend on two fundamental principles. The first is that the computer's cathode-ray-tube, or CRT, monitor is divided into a fine grid of numbered points, much like coordinates on a map. Any location on the monitor—or map—can be found by counting grid squares up or down, left or right. The second is that anything appearing on the screen as a computer graphic—a shape, a color, a reflection or a shadow—begins as a set of numbers such as this: 49 , 9,139,79 ,40,40.

Graphics software in the computer's memory translates this sequence, including the spaces and commas it contains, into binary ones and zeros that a microprocessor can interpret. The results zip through the computer's circuits at dazzling speed. Within microseconds, the software parses the "sentence": Draw a rectangle and fill it with color (40,). Use red (9,). Start at a point on the screen 139 grid units from the left edge and 79 units from the bottom. Make the rectangle 40 units wide and 40 units tall. The result is a bright red square in the center of the monitor. This series of numbers makes sense to a desktop computer of a certain type, loaded with a particular graphics program and connected to a television-like monitor. To other computers loaded with different software and perhaps connected to another type of monitor, the numbers would be unintelligible.

Whatever numbers a program understands can be entered into the computer in many ways. A red square painted on paper might be scanned by a special camera that feeds a signal into an analog-to-digital converter. The digital numbers thus produced are fed into the computer, which stores them in memory. Commands issued to the computer from the keyboard—or through input devices such as a digitizing tablet, a mouse or a light pen *(pages 18-21)*—might be used to tell the computer to display an object described by previously stored numbers.

THE IMAGELESS EARLY DAYS

In the early days of computers, writing a program was the only way to communicate with the machines. Data was fed into computers on punched cards or paper tape, an idea dating back to 1804, when Joseph Marie Jacquard invented an automated loom that used punched cards to control the pattern of the cloth it produced. This was a tremendous laborsaving device, allowing the operator to change designs simply by inserting a different set of cards.

Early digital computers had nothing so elegant as a loom to display results. Output was generally by way of teletype printers. A few computers employed oscilloscope-like devices, but these were used to diagnose internal electronic ailments rather than for any esthetic display. Such limitations did not prevent some computer operators from experimenting, however. Around 1950, for example, an anonymous operator on the EDSAC (Electronic Delay Storage Automatic Computer) at England's Cambridge University produced an image of a Highland dancer on one of the computer's oscilloscopes. About a year and a half

All digital computers use two-state, or binary, logic to process information in basic units called bits and bytes. A bit is the smallest possible unit; it is represented by either of the binary digits 1 or 0, which may signify, for example, whether a current is on or off. A byte is a group of eight bits that generally represents the code for a single letter or numeral.

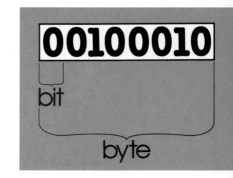

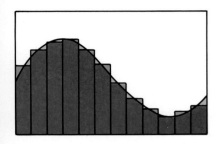

Most input and output processes in a computer involve the translation of analog signals into digital ones, or vice versa. An analog signal is a smoothly changing physical variable, such as light or sound; a digital signal is made up of distinct units such as on-off pulses of electricity. The smooth analog curve shown above can be translated into a digital curve by frequent sampling of its signal at discrete points.

later, the British computer scientist Christopher Strachey programmed the Mark I at the University of Manchester to play a game of checkers on its screen.

But these were isolated instances, more the result of programmers' off-hours tinkering than serious efforts to use the computer's capacity to generate images. In the United States, however, scientists were putting the finishing touches on an innovative computer that would score a number of firsts in the field, not the least of which was an intentional incorporation of graphics in its design.

CONVERSATION WITH A WHIRLWIND

On a Sunday afternoon in December 1951, viewers of the television program *See It Now* listened raptly as newscaster Edward R. Murrow spoke. "These are days of mechanical and electronic marvels," he said. "The Massachusetts Institute of Technology has developed a new one for the Navy." This latest wonder, Murrow told his audience, was the Whirlwind electronic computer. "With considerable trepidation," he went on, "we undertake to interview this new machine. Now to M.I.T. and the computer laboratory in Cambridge, Massachusetts."

The next thing viewers saw on their screens was what seemed to be a neat array of lights flashing a greeting. HELLO MR. MURROW, said the lights. But they were not really lights at all, in the then-conventional sense of the word. They were little points of brilliance positioned to spell out the message on the Whirlwind's CRT. Thus began the public's introduction to the new world of computer graphics.

M.I.T. engineer Jay W. Forrester, microphone and earphone cables trailing stiffly from beneath his jacket, put this curious invention through some of its paces. From his New York studio, Murrow spoke by telephone with a Pentagon-based Navy admiral who posed a problem of the kind that the machine had been built to solve. It involved computations of the fuel consumption, trajectory and velocity of the Viking rocket, which was designed to reach an altitude of about 135 miles before plummeting back to earth. As viewers and a slightly bemused Murrow looked on, Whirlwind's screen glowed with a graph, composed of the same kind of dots as the greeting, that represented the rocket's path, speed and fuel consumption while on a typical flight. "I didn't understand the question," Murrow confessed when it was all over, "and I don't understand the answer."

For later generations, jaded by elaborate video arcade games and the complex special effects achieved by computer graphics in films and television, it is difficult to understand such puzzlement or to grasp the significance of the rather primitive images Whirlwind produced. But the people who watched Murrow's show that Sunday had in fact witnessed the birth of a new medium, one that would seem commonplace in the world of their children.

Whirlwind's public debut had been preceded by several years of intense, groundbreaking labor by the computer's designers. It had all begun in 1944, when Jay Forrester was working in M.I.T.'s Servomechanisms Laboratory, which was doing research on remote-control antiaircraft guns. The facility was headed by Professor Gordon Brown, a brilliant and iconoclastic leader whose unconventional style fostered intellectual independence and promoted a lively esprit de corps within the lab. It was an unusually freewheeling atmosphere in the generally structured academic world of the 1940s. An important element in Brown's philosophy was the notion that his students should have a sense of the practicalities of real-world engineering projects rather than just a theoretical, academic

From Numbers to Images

For tens of thousands of years, artists have known how to carve, paint or draw directly on a flat surface to create images that represent objects from the real world. But creating an image with a computer requires an additional skill; before the machine can render the artist's ideas on a screen or a page, the ideas must be translated into numbers, the only terms computers can understand. Even the most complex computer graphics systems rely on a simple technique—worked out long before there were computers—for representing two-dimensional images as numbers.

In analytic geometry, developed by the French philosopher and mathematician René Descartes in the 17th Century, the

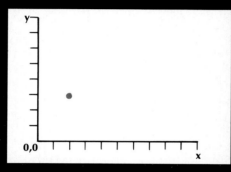

In a Cartesian coordinate system, a point is defined, or mapped, according to its distance, measured in arbitrary units, from the intersection of the horizontal x-axis and the vertical y-axis, whose coordinates are (0,0). In this example, a point with coordinates $x = 2$ and $y = 3$ is mapped by counting two units horizontally and three units vertically from the point (0,0).

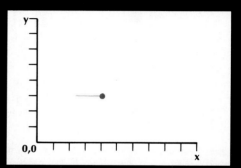

A point is moved by adding to or subtracting from the value of one or both of its coordinates. Here, the point is moved two units to the right by adding 2 to its x-coordinate; the new x-coordinate is 4. Because the y-coordinate is not changed, there is no vertical motion. The point in this example thus moves from (2,3) to (4,3).

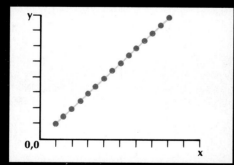

The illusion of a continuous line is created by inserting several evenly spaced points between two endpoints, mapped here at (1,1) and (8,8). The coordinates of the intermediate points are derived by adding a constant value to the coordinates of each successive point. The first of the 13 intermediate points above is mapped at (1.5,1.5); the midpoint of the line is at (4.5,4.5).

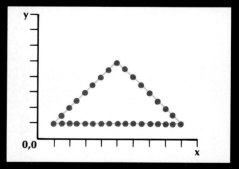

A simple closed figure such as the triangle above is created by mapping the three points that mark the corners of the figure, then mapping the points of the lines that connect them. The endpoints of this triangle are (1,1), (5,5) and (9,1).

location of any point on a plane can be specified by a pair of numbers, or coordinates. Coordinates are determined by measuring the distance to a given point from each of two reference lines that intersect at right angles. Traditionally, the horizontal reference line is called the x-axis, the vertical line is called the y-axis and the point of intersection, or origin, is the zero point. Coordinates are commonly expressed in the form (x,y); thus the coordinates of the point of origin are (0,0). Using Cartesian coordinates, any two-dimensional image can be reduced to a list of the coordinates of the points that make up the image; conversely, given the reference lines and a scale, a list of coordinates can be turned into an image.

Descartes's analytic geometry showed that lines and curves could be described by mathematical equations expressed in terms of x and y. For example, the equation $x - y = 4$ yields a straight line, while $x^2 - 4y = 0$ generates a parabola. Although the principles of Cartesian geometry are demonstrated below with straight lines, even the most complicated shapes are susceptible to mathematical expression.

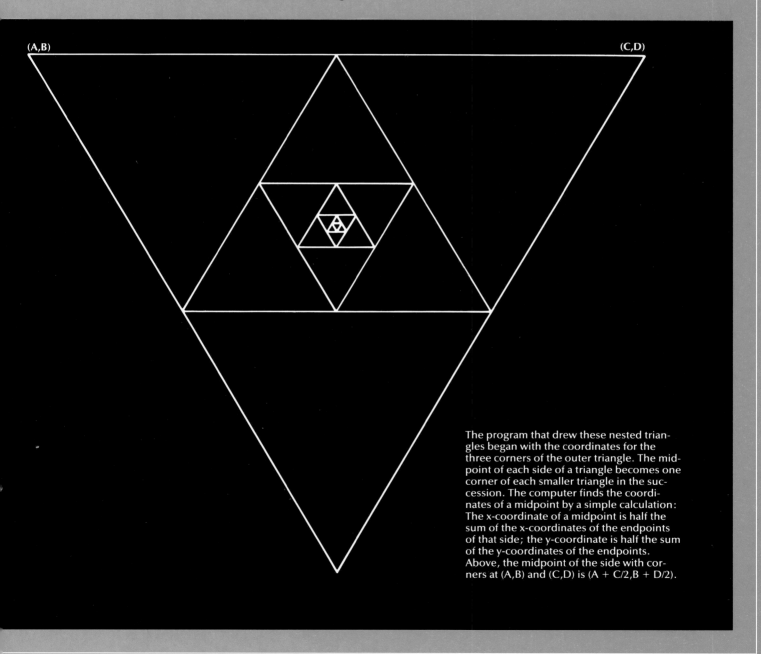

(A,B)　　　　　　　　　　　　　　　　　　　　　(C,D)

The program that drew these nested triangles began with the coordinates for the three corners of the outer triangle. The midpoint of each side of a triangle becomes one corner of each smaller triangle in the succession. The computer finds the coordinates of a midpoint by a simple calculation: The x-coordinate of a midpoint is half the sum of the x-coordinates of the endpoints of that side; the y-coordinate is half the sum of the y-coordinates of the endpoints. Above, the midpoint of the side with corners at (A,B) and (C,D) is (A + C/2,B + D/2).

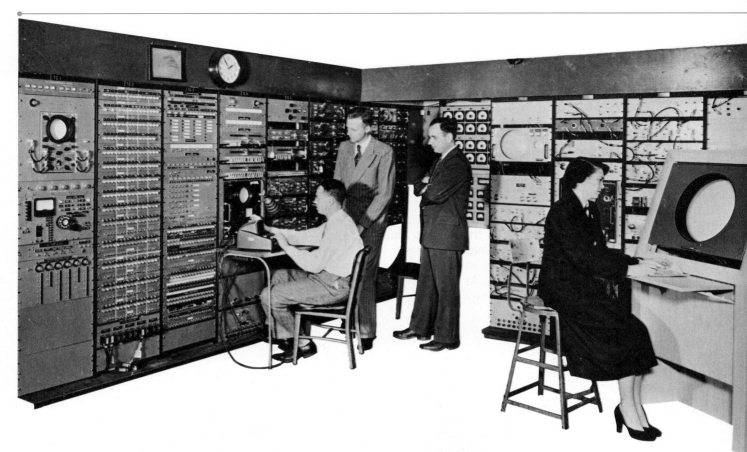

understanding. His tenets and vision had a powerful effect on those who worked with him and carried over into the pioneering spirit that would come to characterize the Whirlwind project.

In the mid-1940s, Brown picked Jay Forrester—a young and somewhat aloof engineer who had already been in charge of several minor efforts at the lab—to lead a team to work on the design of a Navy flight trainer/aircraft-stability analyzer. The equipment was to contain both a cockpit and a large computer, and would be used to train pilots as well as to test the aerodynamics of new aircraft designs. Forrester's group was to concentrate on the project's computer component, which was ultimately to become the Whirlwind. It would be some time before the importance of a graphic display would surface.

Because the computer would be controlling a flight trainer, it had to function at real-time—or instantaneous—speeds that would enable it to respond immediately to the operator's actions. At first, Forrester planned to build a sophisticated analog computer, a machine that would perform its calculations by mechanical means. But a conversation with another engineer in October 1945 convinced him that a high-speed electronic digital computer would be a far better bet.

Although a team at the University of Pennsylvania was working on a pair of such machines, no digital computers had actually been completed. Some components were available from companies that had been meeting the wartime demand for electronic equipment, but many parts and instruments had to be designed and built from scratch.

As Forrester and his staff became more involved in the project, the Whirlwind computer began to eclipse the original flight trainer. Whirlwind was the world's first real-time digital computer, and Forrester realized that it could be used as a general-purpose machine in a number of different systems. By 1948, the Navy

Project chief Jay W. Forrester *(standing, left)* observes the Whirlwind team at work in M.I.T.'s computer control room in the early 1950s. Whirlwind's "bouncing ball" program *(below)* was the first graphic demonstration of data processing in real time.

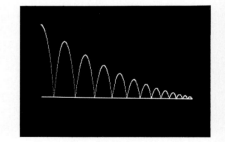

had agreed to shift the project's emphasis, but it gradually tired of being the sole source of funds for the broadening project.

Luckily for Whirlwind, before the end of the decade the United States Air Force was growing concerned about the country's air-defense capabilities. A holdover from the prenuclear, prejet days of World War II, the air-defense system then in place was hopelessly out of date, made up of separate sectors, each with its own radar. The possibility of low-flying attackers posed a special threat; radar range is very short at low altitudes, and data from many radar stations had to be combined to cover large areas. But there was no efficient way to centralize radar information, and recording, analyzing and coordinating it was still more or less a manual task. As the data increased, the speed and efficiency of the operators performing this task became more crucial. Adding urgency to the situation, the Soviet Union had only recently tested its first atomic weapons and had developed long-range bombers that were capable of penetrating American airspace. The United States' air-defense system was totally inadequate to meet such a threat.

At this juncture, Forrester met with George E. Valley, also of M.I.T., who had been helping the Air Force seek a solution to the air-defense problem—and who had characterized the existing system as "lame, purblind and idiot-like." Whirlwind was running by then, and Valley saw that the computer, with its high-speed processing capacity, could be the answer to the Air Force's prayers. The Navy would gradually bow out as the Air Force stepped in with additional funding.

By this time, Forrester's staff had been detached from the Servomechanisms Lab to form M.I.T.'s new Digital Computer Laboratory. The group had been focusing more and more of its attention on such applications as gunfire control, antisubmarine warfare and air-traffic control—all areas that could benefit from a graphic display that would permit an operator to identify targets instantly without having to interpret coordinates on a map. Now, the Digital Lab team began to apply its expertise in air-traffic control to the related area of air defense.

PLOTTING DATA ON THE SCREEN

To receive information on aircraft penetrating American airspace, Whirlwind was linked via telephone lines with a radar station at Hanscom Field, in Bedford, Massachusetts. Traditional radar sets display the position of a target relative to the radar antenna, in the center of the screen. However, to manage air defense over a large area, which might require multiple radar sites, a Whirlwind operator would need a different view of the situation, preferably one in which aircraft were plotted automatically on a map.

This seemingly modest requirement marked the first time that a graphic display of computer data, produced in real time, was specifically requested. Whirlwind programmers wrote a set of instructions to manipulate a series of numbers representing screen coordinates; the computer then translated the numbers into a rough outline of eastern Massachusetts. Upon receiving a radar blip from Hanscom over the phone line, the program converted the radar position to a geographic position, then superimposed the blip on the map shown on the monitor.

This was all straightforward enough. But the problem remained of coming up with a fast and effective way for the operator to react to the incoming information. Robert Everett, Forrester's assistant, designed a light-gun device that looked rather like a pistol with a barrel of unusually large diameter. The gun contained a photoelectric cell receiver; if the computer operator wanted more information on a particular aircraft, he touched the tip of the gun to the blip on the screen. The gun sent a pulse back to the computer, which instantly displayed relevant data about the aircraft, such as its speed and direction. The operator could designate a given blip as a target by touching it with the light gun and typing in a *T* from the keyboard. Special programs also allowed Whirlwind to keep track of available fighter aircraft and to compute interception courses automatically.

A FLAWLESS DEMONSTRATION

These feats were extraordinary, given the state of computer technology in 1950. Equally extraordinary was the way in which the light gun's response to the display on Whirlwind's monitor made possible direct and instantaneous interaction between operator and machine, something that could never happen with punched cards and yards of paper print-out.

Whirlwind gave its first live demonstration on April 20, 1951. Two Air National Guard pilots took off from Hanscom Field, one of them, in a twin-engine C-45, playing the part of an enemy bomber. The other pilot, in a T-6 trainer, took the role of interceptor. Radar relayed the target craft's position to Whirlwind, which displayed the plane as a dot of light labeled *T* on the screen. Also shown was the interceptor's location, about 40 miles from its intended quarry. When the operator touched the target dot with the light gun, Whirlwind automatically computed an interception course. Another operator then radioed the interceptor pilot Whirlwind's directions, which were displayed on the computer monitor.

In each of three practice runs that day, Whirlwind performed flawlessly, prompting the Air Force to expand the project to test a multioperator system. At the same time, the Air Force proceeded with plans for a nationwide network of 22 air-defense sectors plus one in Canada. Controllers in each sector would monitor air traffic with the aid of a Whirlwind-like computer and could respond to an attack. Three combat centers would coordinate overall defense plans. The system was named SAGE (Semi-Automatic Ground Environment); using Whirlwind as the prototype, Jay Forrester and his staff specified design requirements for the network's computers. Although Whirlwind's primitive graphics capabilities were crude by later standards, SAGE was the first production-model computer system with any kind of interactive graphics built into its design. In time, each sector had 50 or more air-control operators, each with his own workstation containing a keyboard for data entry, a light gun and a display scope housed in a console.

The first SAGE center became operational in the summer of 1958, and the system served its assigned mission for a quarter of a century. When the last of the Whirlwind-based SAGE computers were shut down at the end of 1983—to be replaced by more modern hardware—they were the oldest such machines still operating. They had contributed much to the development of computer technology; probably the single most important achievement in terms of graphics was the original notion of linking the computer to a CRT and a light gun, thus introducing a totally new way of communicating with the machines that were to move into the mainstream of society in the years to come.

But in 1951 all of that was still ahead. It remained for still another bright young man from M.I.T., Ivan Sutherland, to lead computer graphics out of its promising infancy, bringing it to the attention of a much wider audience.

Electronic Tools for Designers and Artists

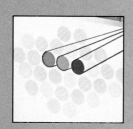

Computer graphics have come a long way in the three decades since scientists working for the military first attempted to display mathematical data on a monitor. The field has expanded far beyond weapons applications into business, entertainment and art, with computer-generated images of a variety and complexity that would astound the early pioneers.

On the hardware side, quantum increases in the processing speed of computers and in the size of their electronic memories have brought about a staggering transformation in the world of computer graphics. The Whirlwind computer of the 1950s could perform 20,000 operations per second; a desktop microcomputer of the mid-1980s works 40 times as fast, and the larger minicomputers used widely in graphics workstations operate even faster. Whirlwind did its job with a memory of only 2,048 bytes—the computer equivalent of about 400 words—compared with the thousands, even millions, of bytes available to its descendants.

Such advances in speed and memory have also made other hardware practical. Early screens, which at their best could produce only green dots and lines that flickered uncertainly, have been replaced by television-like monitors capable of reproducing realistic images in vivid color. Newer monitors, called flat-panel displays, can be large enough to show in their entirety drawings that on most other monitors would be viewed only as a dozen or more segments.

Whirlwind's light gun, invented to select an object on the screen and cause an appropriate response from the computer, survives in a sleeker shape called a light pen. And it has been joined by electronic drawing boards and an instrument engagingly named a mouse that, at a graphics workstation, all but retires the time-honored keyboard from the job of controlling the computer.

Finally, none of these advances in equipment would be so noteworthy were it not for increasingly sophisticated graphics software. When called into play, these essential programs of instructions turn the computer into a powerful and flexible tool for designers and engineers in a host of industries.

A Well-equipped Workstation

Seated at a graphics workstation, facing for the first time an array of electronic hardware, an artist, designer or engineer might well have a question or two: Where are the familiar T squares, compasses and protractors? What of the pens, pencils and paintbrushes? Why are there no eraser crumbs and no wastebasket overflowing with crumpled paper? The very look of the place promises a radically new way of drawing and designing.

And the promise is fulfilled. Software that runs in the computer supplies built-in tools for drawing straight and parallel lines, as well as circles and angles. Ordinary pens, pencils and brushes are antiques, replaced by specialized drawing implements such as the digitizing tablet, the mouse and the light pen *(pages 18-21)*. A new design takes shape on the computer monitor *(pages 22-23)*, where mistakes are corrected electronically, leaving no clue that an error ever existed. Paper is loaded into printers and plotters *(pages 26-27)*, which, along with special cameras *(pages 28-29)*, faultlessly reproduce the final version of a computer image.

A full-featured graphics workstation like the one shown on these pages costs many thousands of dollars. Yet it functions according to the same principles that govern the operation of a workstation centered on a powerful microcomputer *(below)* or even a small home computer of the kind sold in department stores for a few hundred dollars.

Plotter

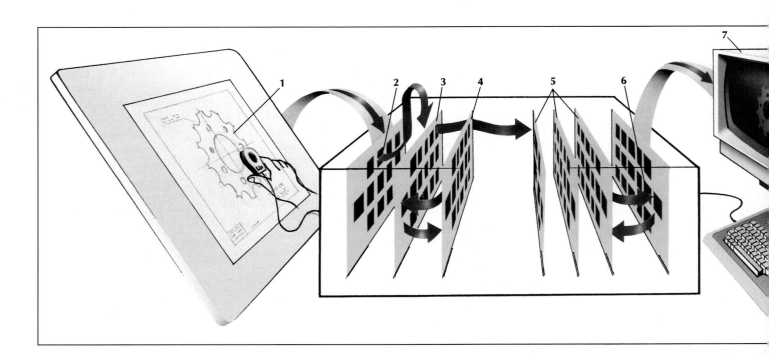

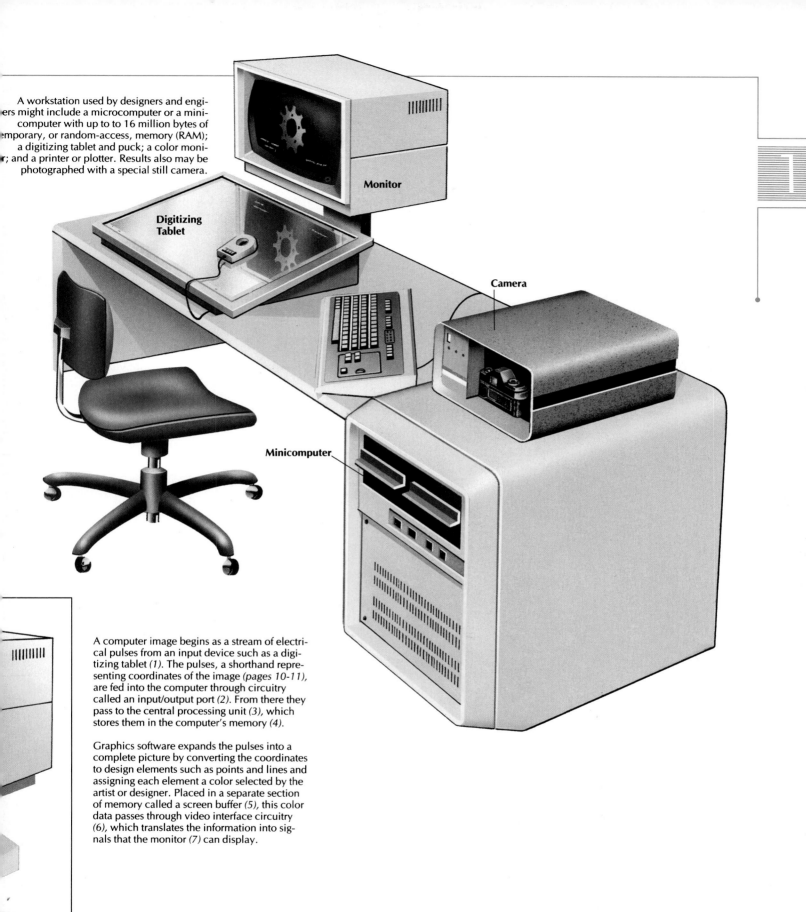

A workstation used by designers and engineers might include a microcomputer or a minicomputer with up to to 16 million bytes of temporary, or random-access, memory (RAM); a digitizing tablet and puck; a color monitor; and a printer or plotter. Results also may be photographed with a special still camera.

Monitor

Digitizing Tablet

Camera

Minicomputer

A computer image begins as a stream of electrical pulses from an input device such as a digitizing tablet *(1)*. The pulses, a shorthand representing coordinates of the image *(pages 10-11)*, are fed into the computer through circuitry called an input/output port *(2)*. From there they pass to the central processing unit *(3)*, which stores them in the computer's memory *(4)*.

Graphics software expands the pulses into a complete picture by converting the coordinates to design elements such as points and lines and assigning each element a color selected by the artist or designer. Placed in a separate section of memory called a screen buffer *(5)*, this color data passes through video interface circuitry *(6)*, which translates the information into signals that the monitor *(7)* can display.

17

Implements for Drawing and Tracing

The graphics tools shown here and on the next two pages offer a way of working with a computer that is more natural to artists and designers than the typing in of commands at the keyboard. In most cases, the software used with these devices allows an artist to call up design elements such as straight lines, arcs, rectangles or circles by selecting the shapes from a list, or menu, that appears on the screen.

A digitizing tablet *(below)*, which is used in conjunction with either a penlike stylus or a flat hand-held device called a puck, may be as small as a sketchpad or as large as a drawing table. With it, an artist can compose images by calling up the shapes provided by the software, by drawing freehand on the tablet or by tracing another image, following the outline with a pair of cross hairs mounted in the puck's window.

A mouse *(page 21)* has most of the digitizing tablet's advantages but at less cost; it will work on any tabletop, saving the expense of the special tablet. Named for its small size and tail of cable leading to the computer, a mouse permits an artist to take advantage of various features of the workstation software and to draw freehand. But because a mouse does not operate on the same principle as a puck, it is not as good at tracing. To copy a drawing without distorting it, an artist would need to hold the mouse perfectly vertical while following the outline, an awkward business compounded by the absence of cross hairs or other aid to accuracy.

Light pens offer an artist or a designer a way to issue instructions to graphics software by, in effect, drawing on the screen. The pen senses patterns of light on the computer screen *(page 20)* rather than beaming rays toward it. Light pens can be used to draw directly on the monitor, move a drawing from one place on the screen to another and select software functions from a menu that appears on the screen.

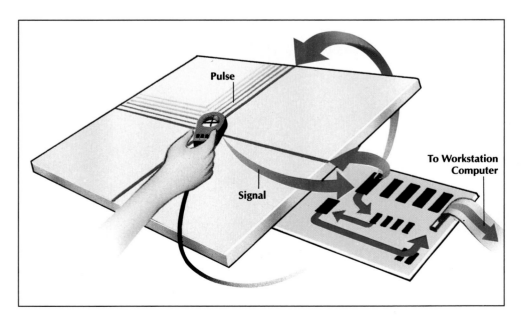

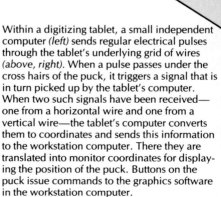

Pulse

Signal

To Workstation Computer

Within a digitizing tablet, a small independent computer *(left)* sends regular electrical pulses through the tablet's underlying grid of wires *(above, right)*. When a pulse passes under the cross hairs of the puck, it triggers a signal that is in turn picked up by the tablet's computer. When two such signals have been received—one from a horizontal wire and one from a vertical wire—the tablet's computer converts them to coordinates and sends this information to the workstation computer. There they are translated into monitor coordinates for displaying the position of the puck. Buttons on the puck issue commands to the graphics software in the workstation computer.

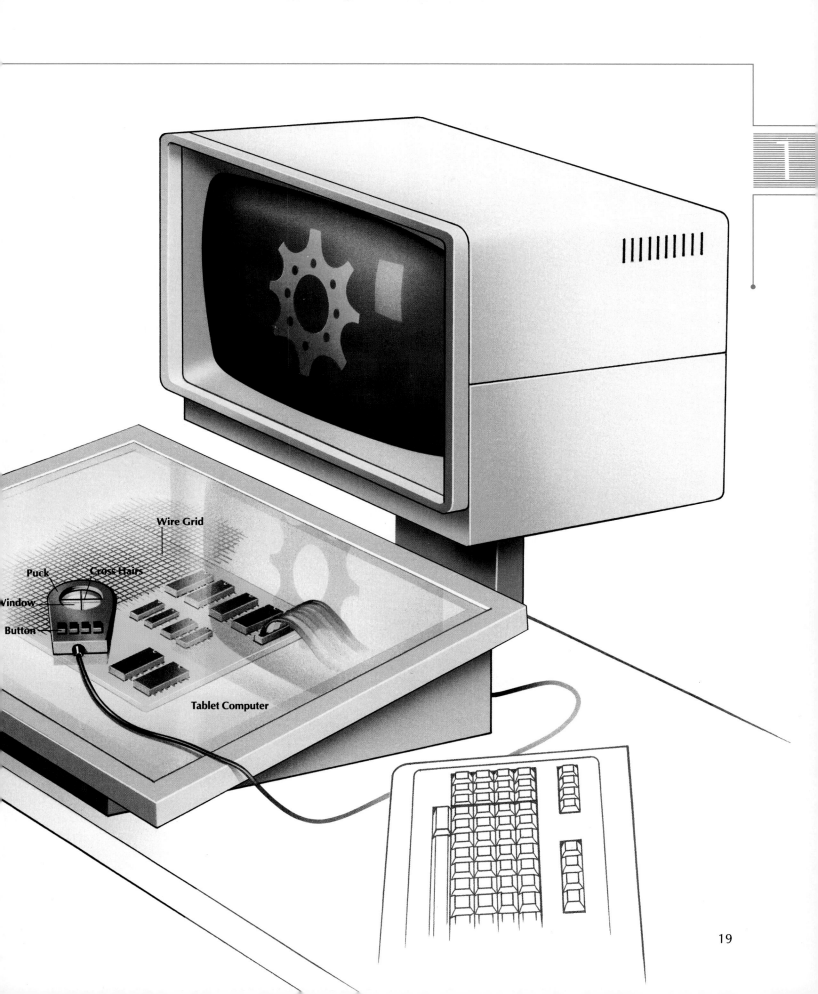

Wire Grid

Puck   Cross Hairs

Window

Button

Tablet Computer

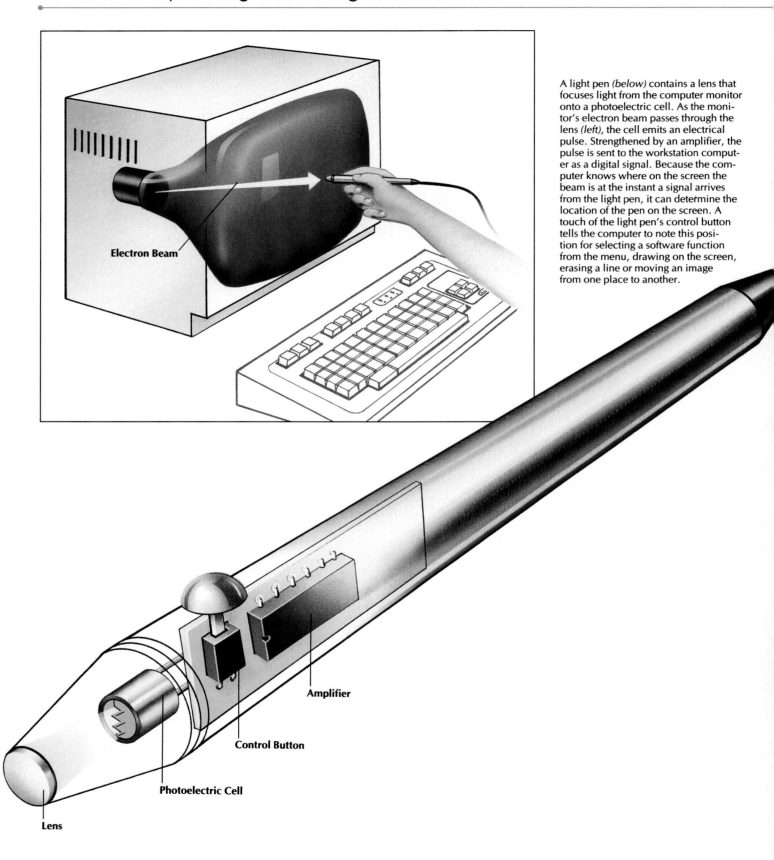

A light pen *(below)* contains a lens that focuses light from the computer monitor onto a photoelectric cell. As the monitor's electron beam passes through the lens *(left)*, the cell emits an electrical pulse. Strengthened by an amplifier, the pulse is sent to the workstation computer as a digital signal. Because the computer knows where on the screen the beam is at the instant a signal arrives from the light pen, it can determine the location of the pen on the screen. A touch of the light pen's control button tells the computer to note this position for selecting a software function from the menu, drawing on the screen, erasing a line or moving an image from one place to another.

Electron Beam

Amplifier

Control Button

Photoelectric Cell

Lens

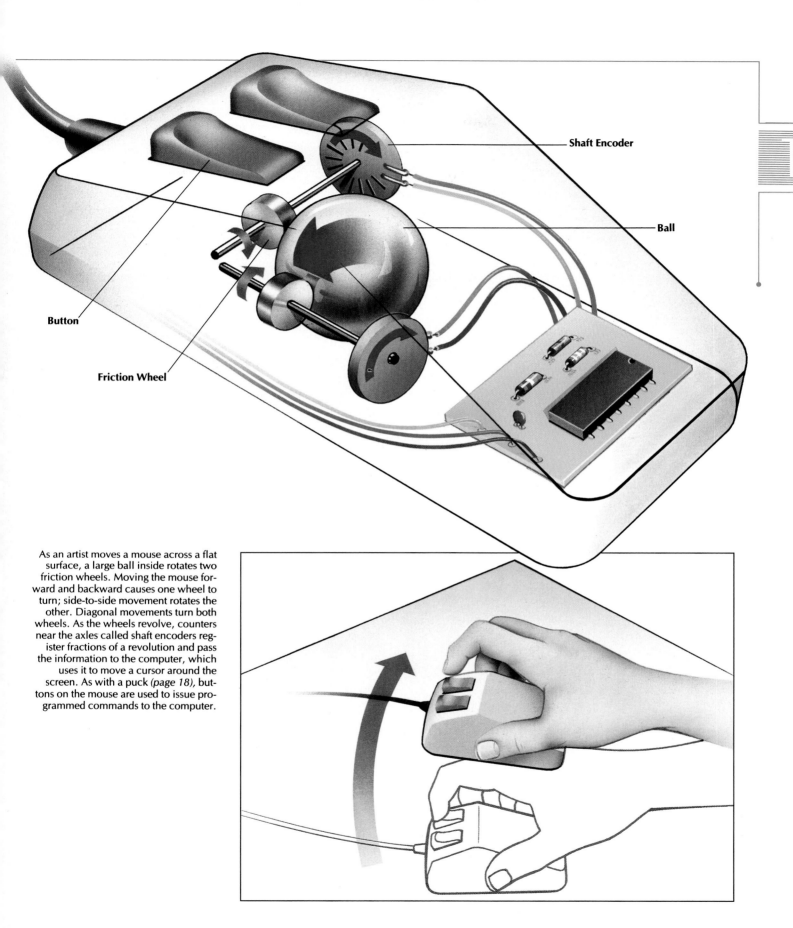

Shaft Encoder

Ball

Button

Friction Wheel

As an artist moves a mouse across a flat surface, a large ball inside rotates two friction wheels. Moving the mouse forward and backward causes one wheel to turn; side-to-side movement rotates the other. Diagonal movements turn both wheels. As the wheels revolve, counters near the axles called shaft encoders register fractions of a revolution and pass the information to the computer, which uses it to move a cursor around the screen. As with a puck (page 18), buttons on the mouse are used to issue programmed commands to the computer.

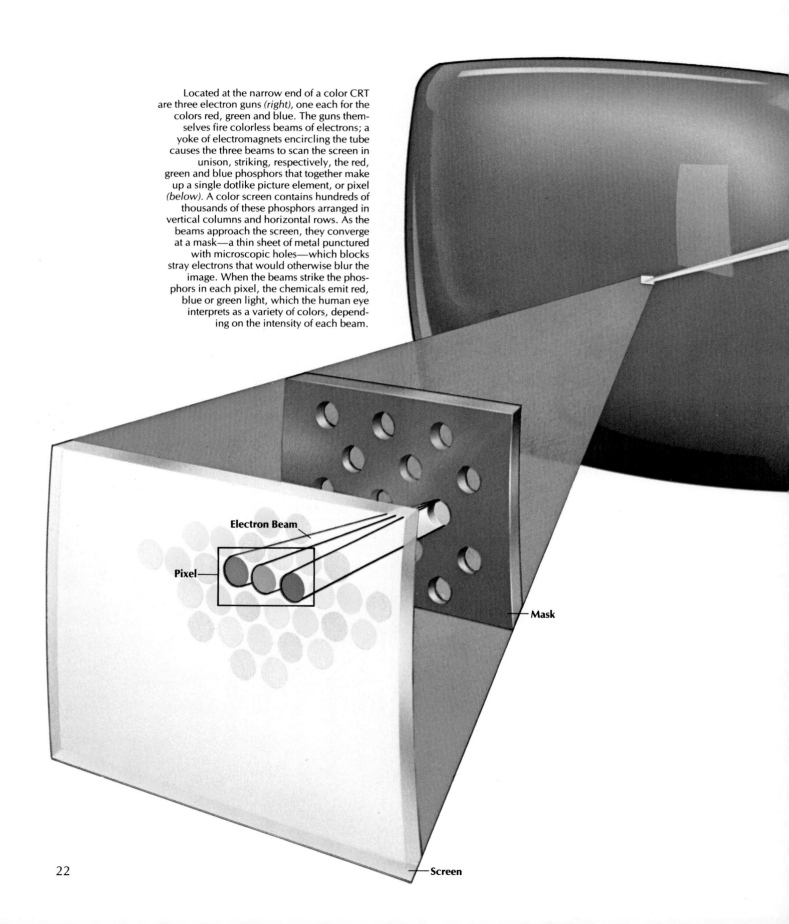

Located at the narrow end of a color CRT are three electron guns *(right)*, one each for the colors red, green and blue. The guns themselves fire colorless beams of electrons; a yoke of electromagnets encircling the tube causes the three beams to scan the screen in unison, striking, respectively, the red, green and blue phosphors that together make up a single dotlike picture element, or pixel *(below)*. A color screen contains hundreds of thousands of these phosphors arranged in vertical columns and horizontal rows. As the beams approach the screen, they converge at a mask—a thin sheet of metal punctured with microscopic holes—which blocks stray electrons that would otherwise blur the image. When the beams strike the phosphors in each pixel, the chemicals emit red, blue or green light, which the human eye interprets as a variety of colors, depending on the intensity of each beam.

Electron Beam

Pixel

Mask

Screen

A Behind-the-screens Look at Monitors

Most monitors used at computer graphics workstations are based on a device invented in the 1930s—the cathode-ray tube, or CRT. A CRT is a sealed glass tube, the wide end of which is coated on the inside with chemicals called phosphors. Phosphors glow when struck by electrons emanating from an electrode, called a gun, in the narrow end. In a raster monitor *(below, left)*, the electron beam scans the entire screen to display an image. A vector monitor *(below)* directs the beam from point to point only.

Because its electron gun is specifically designed to draw lines in this point-to-point fashion, a vector monitor is rarely used to produce images with filled-in surfaces or color. The guns in raster monitors, however, scan every point on the screen and can thus fill in outlines to create solid shapes.

A color monitor capable of displaying realistic images is an important component of graphics workstations for animators and special effects artists. But for other types of tasks the time required for the computer to process color information can be a drawback. Sometimes designers and engineers opt to use a vector monitor, which can display complex diagrams and change them quickly.

Electron Guns

Yoke

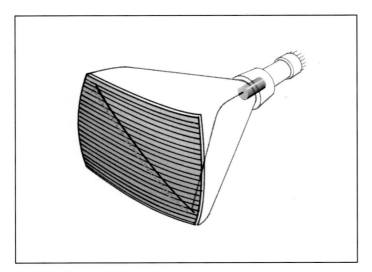

Raster scanning, line by line
The electron beam in a raster monitor scans the screen from left to right and from top to bottom (a color monitor would have three beams), lighting up only designated pixels to form an image—in this case a diagonal line. When the beam reaches the right edge of the tube, it is turned off and returned to the left edge to scan the next line, one pixel lower, refreshing the entire image 30 to 60 times per second.

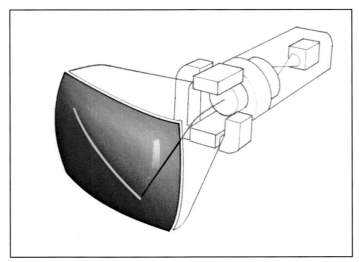

Vector scanning, point to point
The electron beam in a vector monitor forms lines on the screen by moving directly from one set of coordinates to another, lighting up all the phosphors between the two points; thus the screen need not be divided into pixels, which must be turned on or off individually. The technique is faster than the whole-screen raster scan and also requires less memory for storing the image.

A Slender Trio of Flat-Panel Displays

The screen of a flat-panel display, as the name suggests, lacks the subtle curvature of a CRT screen. These displays are comparatively svelte—typically three inches or less from front to back. They range in size from about 108 square inches, or four times the area of the typical personal computer monitor, to monsters of 1,600 square inches. Improvements in technology may make still larger displays, with higher resolution and even color, as widely used as the CRT monitor.

Flat-panel displays employ one of three techniques. Gas plasma monitors, like neon signs, exploit the property of some gases to glow when electricity flows through them. Electroluminescent monitors use phosphorescent compounds similar to those coated inside the screen of a CRT. Liquid crystal displays, familiar from digital watches and pocket calculators, employ the light-bending powers of a family of chemicals called biphenyls.

For all their differences, flat-panel displays have much in common. Each is composed of closely spaced electrodes sandwiched between glass. Stretching across the outer glass panel are rows of transparent electrodes that pass near columns of additional electrodes on the rear glass panel, forming a grid of pixels. Following instructions from the computer, an electric current passes between the electrodes at these points, causing the gas, the phosphor or the liquid crystals to form an image on the screen.

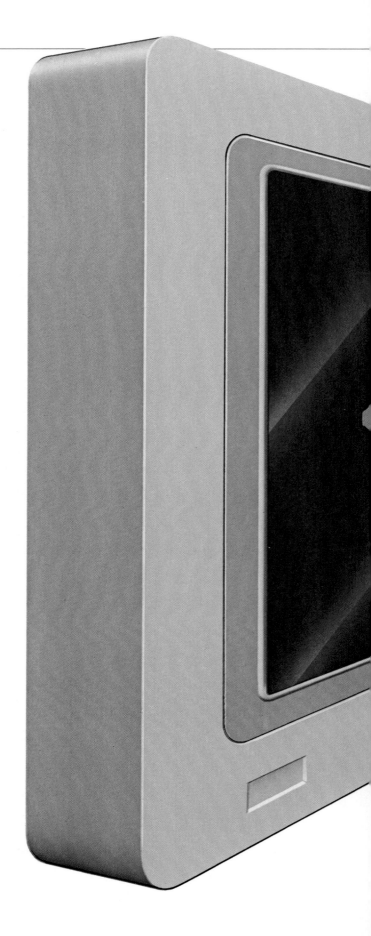

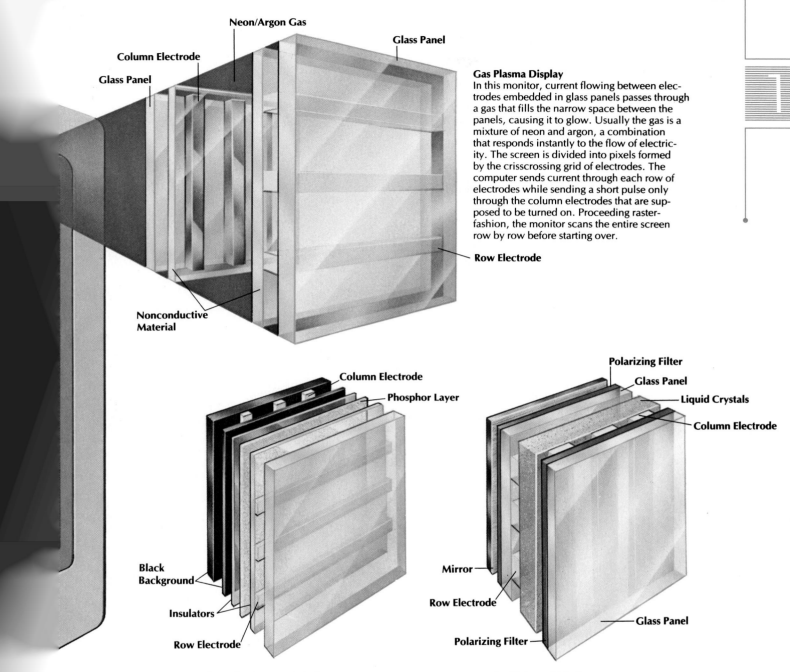

Neon/Argon Gas

Column Electrode

Glass Panel

Glass Panel

Nonconductive Material

Row Electrode

Gas Plasma Display

In this monitor, current flowing between electrodes embedded in glass panels passes through a gas that fills the narrow space between the panels, causing it to glow. Usually the gas is a mixture of neon and argon, a combination that responds instantly to the flow of electricity. The screen is divided into pixels formed by the crisscrossing grid of electrodes. The computer sends current through each row of electrodes while sending a short pulse only through the column electrodes that are supposed to be turned on. Proceeding raster-fashion, the monitor scans the entire screen row by row before starting over.

Column Electrode

Phosphor Layer

Polarizing Filter

Glass Panel

Liquid Crystals

Column Electrode

Black Background

Insulators

Row Electrode

Mirror

Row Electrode

Polarizing Filter

Glass Panel

Electroluminescent Display

An electroluminescent monitor is much like a gas plasma display except that the mixture of neon and argon is replaced by a layer of a phosphorescent substance so thin that it is transparent. Similar to the material used in CRTs, the phosphor layer lights up brilliantly at points where electricity passes between a vertical electrode and a horizontal one. A light-absorbing layer gives the image a dark background.

Liquid Crystal Display

A thin layer of liquid crystals, sandwiched between two polarizing filters and a mirror, acts as a switch to turn a pixel on or off. When the current to a pixel is off, light from the surroundings enters the glass front of the panel, passes both the front and rear polarizing filters, and is reflected by the mirror; the pixel appears gray. If the current to a pixel is turned on, the liquid crystals align themselves so that light entering the top is absorbed by the bottom polarizer and the pixel appears black.

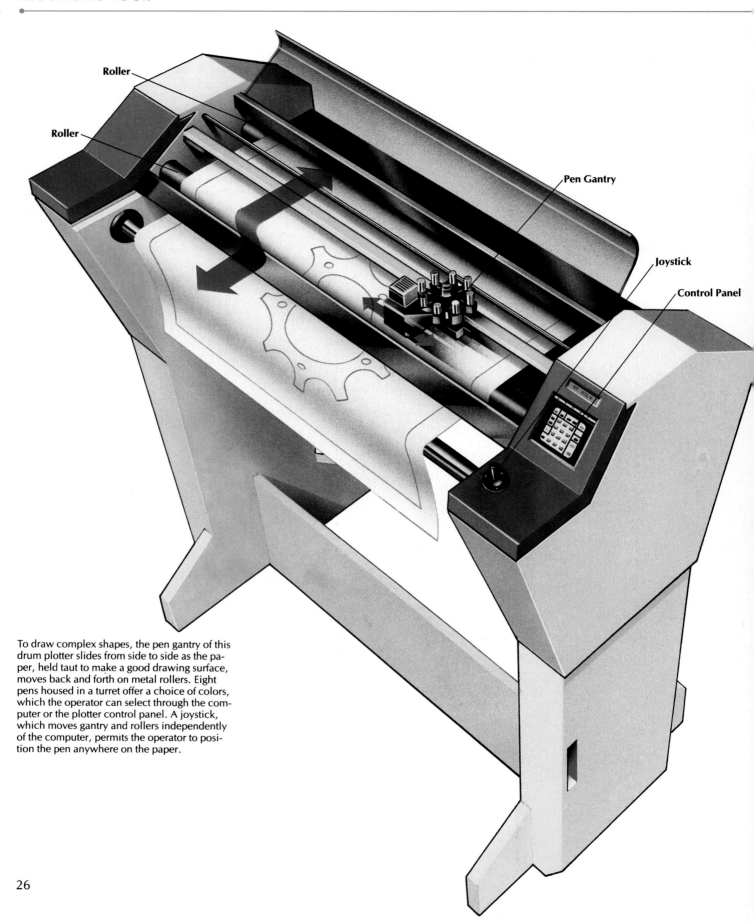

Roller

Roller

Pen Gantry

Joystick

Control Panel

To draw complex shapes, the pen gantry of this drum plotter slides from side to side as the paper, held taut to make a good drawing surface, moves back and forth on metal rollers. Eight pens housed in a turret offer a choice of colors, which the operator can select through the computer or the plotter control panel. A joystick, which moves gantry and rollers independently of the computer, permits the operator to position the pen anywhere on the paper.

Transferring Images to Paper

Printers and plotters, the scribes of graphics workstations, use different techniques to transfer to paper the luminous designs that appear on computer monitors.

Most printers reproduce graphics by depositing ink on the paper as tiny dots. By leaving spaces and printing some dots once, twice or more, the printer forms an image as it scans the paper line by line. Even inexpensive printers can make pictures in tones of gray. Simple color is also possible, by using multicolored ribbons. Far more versatile is the ink jet printer shown below. It can create a palette of 125 colors by combining droplets of yellow, cyan and magenta inks. Because black, when composed of these colors, turns out dark gray, some ink jet printers add black as a fourth color.

Producing black presents no difficulty to a plotter; it draws with a battery of colored pens. Work begins when the plotter sets a pen down on paper at one place and moves it directly to another. Then, according to instructions from the computer, the pen may be switched for one of a different color and a new line begun in a different quadrant of the paper. Plotters are distinguished by the way they handle the paper. In a flatbed, plotter paper is laid out on the base of the machine. For large drawings, a more compact alternative is the drum plotter *(left)*, which has only a small writing surface but shifts the paper as the drawing requires. Plotters are slower than printers, but the results, formed of sharp, unbroken lines and clean colors, are closer to those drawn by hand.

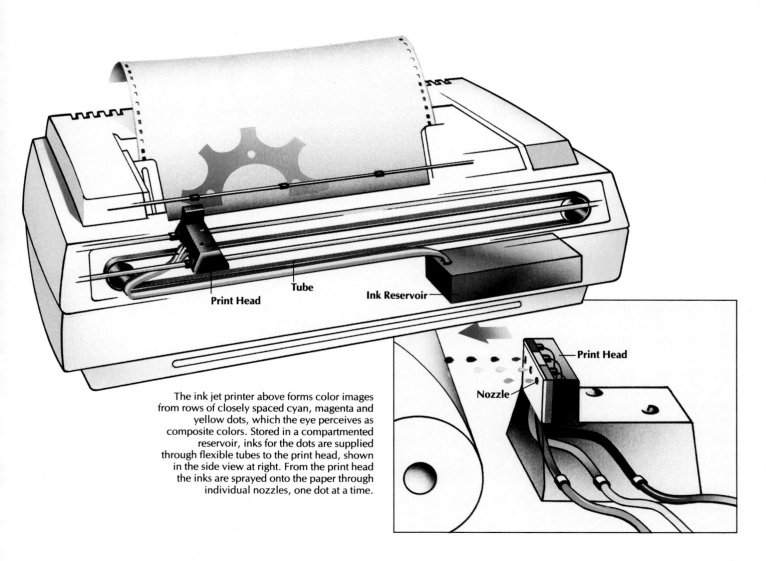

Print Head **Tube** **Ink Reservoir**

Print Head

Nozzle

The ink jet printer above forms color images from rows of closely spaced cyan, magenta and yellow dots, which the eye perceives as composite colors. Stored in a compartmented reservoir, inks for the dots are supplied through flexible tubes to the print head, shown in the side view at right. From the print head the inks are sprayed onto the paper through individual nozzles, one dot at a time.

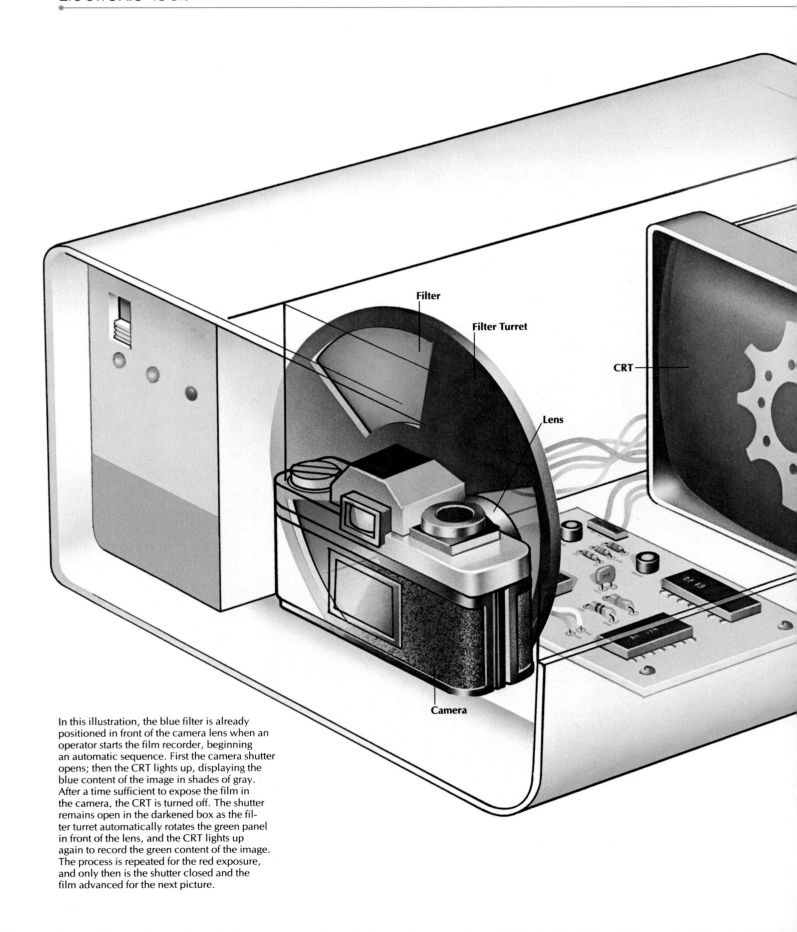

Filter

Filter Turret

CRT

Lens

Camera

In this illustration, the blue filter is already positioned in front of the camera lens when an operator starts the film recorder, beginning an automatic sequence. First the camera shutter opens; then the CRT lights up, displaying the blue content of the image in shades of gray. After a time sufficient to expose the film in the camera, the CRT is turned off. The shutter remains open in the darkened box as the filter turret automatically rotates the green panel in front of the lens, and the CRT lights up again to record the green content of the image. The process is repeated for the red exposure, and only then is the shutter closed and the film advanced for the next picture.

Devices for Filming the Screen

Images on a monitor, no matter how accessible through a keyboard, are prisoners of the computer if they cannot be carried away as hard copy on paper *(pages 26-27)* or film.

A speedy and economical way to photograph a computer image is to shoot a picture of it directly from the monitor with an ordinary 35mm camera. If the camera is attached to a special hood like the one shown below, the resulting photograph will faithfully reproduce an image as it appears on the screen—including the jagged graininess characteristic of color monitors, an effect that may become objectionable if the pictures are subsequently enlarged.

Better results are possible from a film recorder. This device displays the red, blue and green components of a color image as tones of gray on a black-and-white monitor having up to five times the resolution of most color monitors. A triple exposure through colored filters reassembles the image on film in full color—and with such clarity that it can be enlarged to auditorium scale. The film recorder shown at left accepts a specially modified 35mm camera. Others are designed to work with movie cameras, taking the film recorder into the realm of animation and special effects.

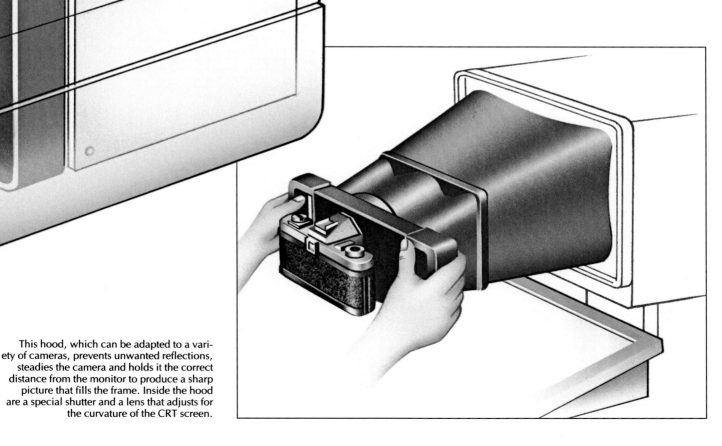

This hood, which can be adapted to a variety of cameras, prevents unwanted reflections, steadies the camera and holds it the correct distance from the monitor to produce a sharp picture that fills the frame. Inside the hood are a special shutter and a lens that adjusts for the curvature of the CRT screen.

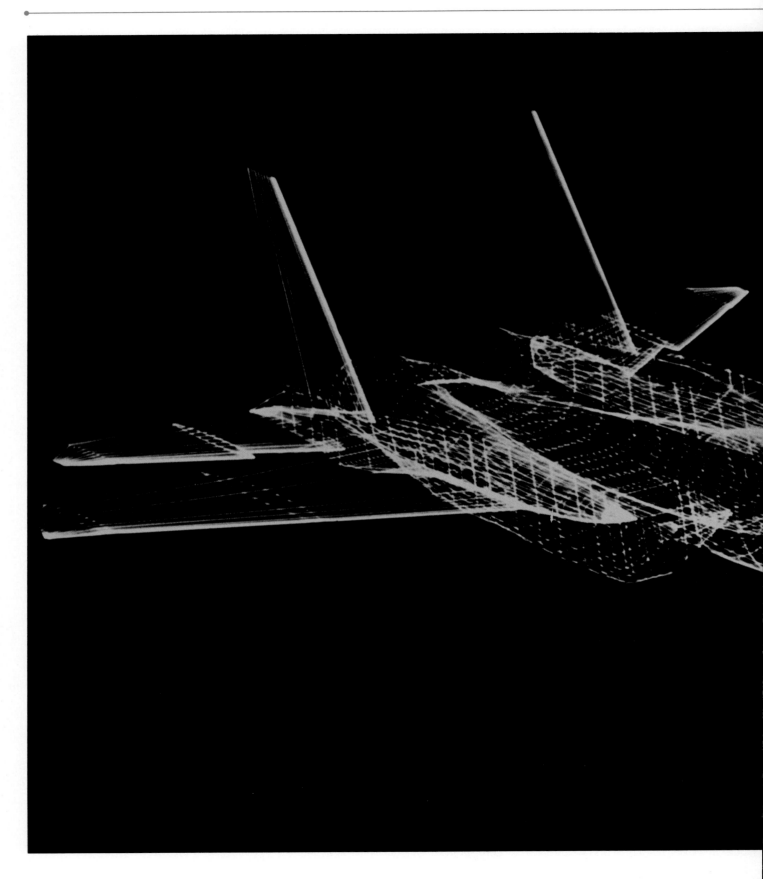

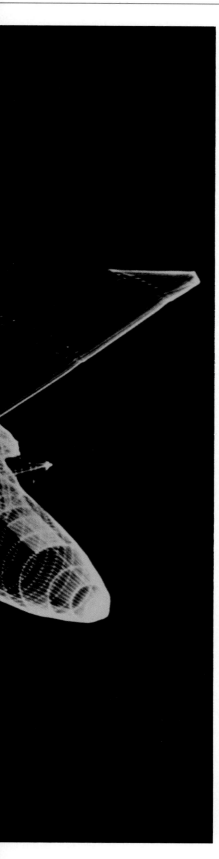

Toward a Machine with Interactive Skills

While Boston and its environs slept away the predawn hours of a November morning in 1961, Ivan Sutherland, doctoral candidate in electrical engineering at the Massachusetts Institute of Technology and computer programmer extraordinary, sat engrossed at the console of the TX-2 computer in the basement of M.I.T.'s Lincoln Laboratory. He was at work on his dissertation project, a computer drawing program he called Sketchpad. The name derived from the proclivity of engineers to rough out an idea on a scrap of paper, then gradually refine it by making innumerable revisions. Sutherland was convinced that he could turn the computer into a superior tool for this process.

Sutherland was only one of many researchers captivated by the interactive possibilities of the TX-2, so he had to scramble for a share of the computer's precious time, even if that meant getting out of bed at two or three in the morning. The solitude of his sessions at the computer did not bother the 23-year-old Sutherland; in some ways it suited his personality. Brilliant and idiosyncratic, he was known as a man who went his own way. He could focus his formidable powers of concentration and shut out anything extraneous. "It wasn't that he was unfriendly," an acquaintance explained; "he just zeroed in on whatever he was involved in. If you were at his house and it was time for him to go to bed, he would get up and excuse himself and tell you to lock up when you left. That was just his way."

On that November morning, Sutherland's left hand hovered over a box studded with closely spaced push buttons. In his right he held a light pen that resembled the light gun invented more than a decade earlier and used on the Whirlwind computer. Sutherland held the tip of the light pen to the center of a computer monitor, where he had programmed the word "ink" to appear. At the touch of the pen, the word was replaced by a small cross. Sutherland then

Stripped to structural basics, an Air Force F-15 jet fighter is shown as a three-dimensional wire-frame model on a high-resolution vector monitor. Vector displays are used by designers and engineers in many fields to isolate and clearly identify components.

punched one of the push buttons and began to move the light pen. As he did so, a bright green line appeared, stretching from the center of the cross to the pen's new position. Wherever he moved the pen, the line followed, like a rubber band with one end tacked to the center of the cross and the other attached to the pen. With a second push-button command, the line remained frozen on the screen as Sutherland moved the light pen away.

Modest as it may seem a quarter of a century later, the line was proof of an extraordinary accomplishment. In a stroke, Sutherland had extended the practical applications of interaction between human and computer. Sketchpad was a masterly synthesis of two different branches of developmental effort. The first was work done by programmers on the TX-2 and its predecessor, the TX-0, to develop software that gave these machines limited line-drawing capabilities. Sutherland also utilized programming techniques invented for the APT (Automatically Programmed Tools) System, an early computer-aided manufacturing system that used a computer to control tools for milling pieces of equipment.

Realizing that computer graphics could have significant applications in engineering and design, Sutherland bent his efforts toward increasing the operator's control of the image on the screen. Where an operator at the TX-2 could draw simple shapes on the screen with a light pen, the shape could not be manipulated. "In the past," Sutherland explained in the technical report on Sketchpad that M.I.T. published in January 1963, "we have been writing letters to rather than conferring with our computers."

In contrast, Sketchpad promised to turn the computer into a tool that anyone might use. Even at this early stage, the program allowed someone with no programming experience to solve complex engineering problems through the

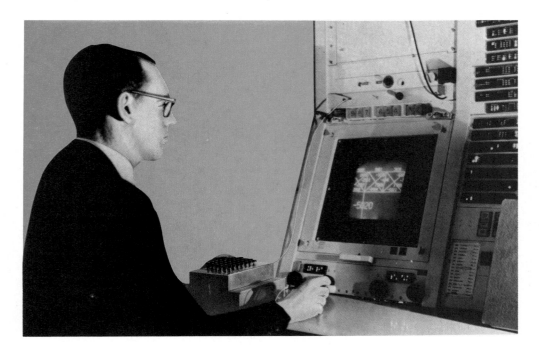

Sitting at the console of the Lincoln Lab TX-2 computer, programmer Ivan Sutherland uses the Sketchpad graphics program to manipulate a bridge design. This pioneering interactive program, devised by Sutherland in 1961, enabled users not only to draw and erase on the screen but also to demonstrate the results of engineering tests. Commands were entered with the light pen in Sutherland's hand and the push buttons to his left.

use of computer graphics. In effect, Sketchpad translated the operator's wishes into the computer's binary language and displayed the machine's response instantly, in real time.

Sutherland's work at M.I.T. would ultimately be viewed as heralding a crucial turning point in the history of computer graphics. Before Sutherland and Sketchpad, most of the graphics applications of computers were for military purposes and were relatively crude. After Sutherland, computer graphics was used increasingly as a tool for industrial engineering and design, primarily in the auto and aerospace industries but gradually in others as well. Largely because of Sutherland's skill and vision, computer graphics moved into the world beyond the laboratory and the military base.

EN ROUTE TO A SIMPLE LINE

Sutherland had first decided to write a computer graphics program in April of 1961. The preceding winter, while working on other projects, he had become familiar with the TX-2 and noticed that its design made drawing convenient. Besides the light pen, it had a CRT screen and enough memory to hold 280,000 bytes, a prodigious capacity at the time. Furthermore, the TX-2 could be modified with little difficulty, and Sutherland requested the addition of a bank of push buttons. Work on Sketchpad began in earnest in the fall of 1961. An early success was to make a small cross displayed on the computer monitor follow the light pen obediently around the screen. The cross provided a signal for the light pen to detect and lock onto, and served as the starting point for a drawing. To accomplish this, Sutherland wrote a program instructing the computer to draw the cross, centered on the pair of coordinates *(pages 10-11)* closest to the tip of the light pen. To make the cross respond to the pen's movement, the program analyzed signals generated when the pen touched any part of the cross; the signals determined where the pen lay in relation to the cross's center. If the pen had moved, the program redrew the cross, centering it at new coordinates nearest to the tip of the pen. Repeated hundreds of times each second, these steps took place so rapidly that the cross appeared to tag along after the light pen as the pen was moved from one point to another on the screen.

Sutherland had to program a score of other details before Sketchpad could draw a simple straight line. For example, he wrote instructions to the computer that interpreted pushing a button as an order to remember the coordinates of the cross's position at that instant. Another subprogram directed the computer to calculate a new set of points lying on a straight line between the initial fixed point and the point to which the light pen might be moved. This subprogram also interpreted a second push-button command as an instruction to end the line. A third routine stored the line in a portion of the TX-2's memory called the refresh buffer. The computer retrieved lines from the refresh buffer and redrew them 20 times a second to keep them from fading.

Sutherland was just getting started. Even though Sketchpad could draw straight lines, it knew nothing of curves, essential forms if the program were ever to be of service to engineers and draftsmen. Sutherland first simplified the problem by limiting the program's curves to circular arcs. To draw an arc or a complete circle, the operator would tell Sketchpad with one push-button command where the center of the circle was to lie, then move the pen and push the button a second time, thus defining the length of the radius and telling Sketchpad where to begin drawing. At that point, the program would produce an arc until a third command halted the process.

Not until mid-1962 could Sketchpad draw a portion of a circle that was larger than the screen—a feature necessary for making shallow curves. In effect, Sutherland had to make the edge of the screen disappear for the computer. He did it by establishing phantom coordinates beyond the screen's perimeter. As long as the radius of a circle was less than the width of the screen, the TX-2 could draw the circle, although only the part that fit on the screen would be displayed.

DEFINING OBJECTS WITH RULES

Still to be programmed into Sketchpad were routines that Sutherland called constraints, the rules for manipulating a drawing. At this stage in the program's development, drawing a shape such as a square was akin to laying out matchsticks on a table. Even if the operator could draw four lines of equal length, arranging them perpendicular to one another was difficult. Nonetheless, the result was merely four lines in the shape of a square; repositioning the square would ruin it as surely as if it had indeed been made of matchsticks.

Sketchpad's constraints allowed an operator to create an object by defining its properties. A square might begin as a rough, four-sided figure, but the operator could then instruct the program always to keep the lines joined in a closed shape, to make them equal in length and to keep all four angles locked at 90 degrees. Thereafter, if one side of the square was moved on the screen, the other sides would be forced to come along in order to obey the constraints associated with that shape.

These rules and others that Sutherland later programmed into Sketchpad were to give computer drawing its great potential. A Sketchpad drawing would consist of points, lines and arcs linked together to form objects. Once created, any object, or shape, could be enlarged, reduced or rotated on the screen. It could be stored in a library of shapes and recalled for future use. It could be duplicated and the copies arranged to generate a new shape. With these rules, a complex drawing of a bridge or an automobile could be created as a hierarchy of simpler components, each of which could be altered and moved around on the screen.

As is often the case with innovative software, little of Sutherland's programming operated perfectly at first. "The trials of getting systems to work are many," he wrote later. One memorable trial concerned rotating an object on the screen. If, for example, a small figure were drawn inside a larger one and linked with it to make a single object, then rotating the outer image to the right should have caused the inner one to turn in the same direction. Perversely, the small figure revolved to the left. After tedious hours of debugging, Sutherland unmasked the problem: He had transposed some positive and negative values.

"By Memorial Day, 1962," continued Sutherland, "it was possible to see that sketching could indeed be done on the computer." One early test was to produce graph paper based not on squares but on hexagons. Within an hour after beginning work, Sutherland had linked 900 identical hexagons edge to edge, and a flat-bed plotter connected to the computer had drawn a 30-inch-

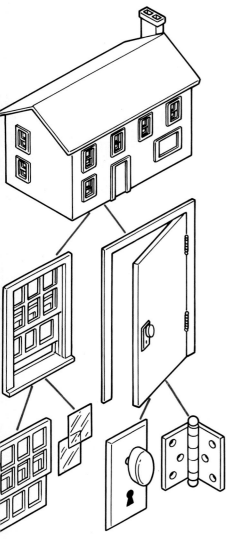

A graphic data base—the computer files containing all of an image's basic elements—is frequently organized in the so-called tree structure shown here. Conceived by Ivan Sutherland for his Sketchpad program, such data bases allow quick access to information by storing data in major sets, each containing subsets. For example, to call a door hinge onto the screen the operator would look for "door" as a major set within the "house" data base, and "hinge" as a subset within "door."

by-30-inch master of the pattern. "Professional draftsmen," noted Sutherland, "estimated that it would take them two days to produce a similar pattern." Sketchpad was at last demonstrating the speed and agility that Sutherland had envisioned.

AN INSPIRATIONAL EFFECT

About this time, Sutherland made a movie of Sketchpad in operation. He showed it around the M.I.T. campus to students and teachers, soliciting their opinions. Copies of the film made their way to other campuses. David Evans, who later joined Sutherland in founding a computer graphics company, was then a computer science and electrical engineering professor at the University of California at Berkeley. He remembers that the Sketchpad film was "like an underground movie. There were lots of copies around. It was immediately obvious that this was beyond what anyone else had done. It was elegant."

The Sketchpad film debuted at the spring Joint Computer Conference in Detroit in 1963, where it fired the imaginations of those who had not yet seen it. Andries van Dam, later chairman of the Brown University computer science department, was one of them. He decided "on the spot that graphics was going to be my research area." Van Dam shared Sutherland's opinion that Sketchpad's most immediate value lay in designing new products. An electronics engineer, for example, might use Sketchpad to create a library of basic circuit components such as transistors and resistors, then combine them into amplifiers, motor-control circuits and other useful devices.

Nevertheless, the reaction from potential corporate sponsors was disappointing at first. Industry in general seemed to have something of a blind spot when it came to computer graphics, regarding the idea as a bit of impractical electronic razzmatazz. One man who had observed it all from the start—and had experienced the frustrations—was Thurber Moffett, an aeronautical engineer for General Dynamics Corporation in San Diego. In 1955, Moffett had collaborated with an IBM engineer named Robert Cortney to develop an engineering computer system for the Defense Department. Moffett and Cortney spent five months in San Diego working up a proposal. One of their aims was to show engineering data as graphs on the computer screen. But evenings after work, they speculated about matters that went beyond the task at hand. "Bob and I used to have dinner together two or three nights a week at the King's Inn," Moffett recounted, "and we diagramed what we thought an interactive computer graphics system should look like on the tablecloths. We did it just to amuse ourselves. We had no real notion what would come out of it."

Moffett remembered the ho-hum reaction from corporate executives who saw presentations of Sketchpad: "They would look at it and go away thinking that it was some witchcraft, something they did not have to worry about until maybe 2010. There was probably not one in a thousand who realized what Ivan had done."

Among the few who appreciated Sketchpad were the executives of General Motors Corporation. GM, in fact, had been pioneering the idea all along. In 1959, two years before Sutherland began work on Sketchpad, GM entered into a farsighted collaboration with IBM to build a computer system that would facilitate the design of cars. The project was called DAC-1, for Design Augmented by Computers. Like Sutherland, DAC-1's creators wanted to turn the computer into a design tool, but as is common in the world of computers, they arrived at a different solution.

DAC-1 was unveiled in 1964 at the Joint Computer Conference, the same forum that Sutherland had used for Sketchpad a year earlier. Where Sketchpad's repertoire of curves was limited to arcs of circles, DAC-1 could reproduce the flowing lines favored by automobile stylists, even though such curves obey no simple mathematical formulas. But because a car's shape must be drawn more precisely than a draftsman can work freehand, DAC-1 contained no provision like Sketchpad's for creating a design on the screen from scratch. Instead, the system required that a designer either describe the desired shape in a program and feed it into the computer or submit conventional engineering drawings to be read into memory with a digitizing camera. With the drawing in the computer, DAC-1 became more interactive, employing an electronic stylus, much as Sketchpad used a light pen, to permit the operator to enlarge the drawing and change portions of it. GM shied away from describing the system as being able to perform in real time, but in fact, DAC-1 reacted quickly.

Thurber Moffett recalled that people lined up two hours ahead of time to get in to see the DAC-1 demonstration. The technicians operating the machine "showed a structure rotating on the screen," Moffett said. "Nobody had ever seen that before." As Moffett walked from the conference rooms after the demonstration, he heard someone call his name. It was Robert Cortney. Moffett asked his old friend if he had been involved in the GM graphics system. "That's my baby," Cortney replied.

"You son of a gun," Moffett exclaimed, "you saved those tablecloths!"

GM'S SEAL OF APPROVAL

General Motors' commitment to computer graphics proved to be a breakthrough; if a company as big and smart as GM was putting its money on the line, computer graphics had to be more than just an electronic flash in the pan. Lockheed-Georgia went to work on a graphics system to help in the design of airplanes. General Electric, Sperry Rand and TRW all showed interest in exploiting the newly discovered graphic powers of the computer. Oil companies also began work on computer systems for charting data derived from exploratory seismic soundings. By the end of 1964, estimated Carl Machover, a computer graphics consultant, there were perhaps 100 computer graphics terminals in use at various companies and universities. But like DAC-1, they were all one-of-a-kind, custom-designed systems. A company that wanted a ready-made terminal was out of luck.

That situation changed in 1965 when IBM, noting the surge of interest in computer graphics for design and engineering, capitalized on its experience with DAC-1 to bring out the first commercially available computer graphics terminal. Called the IBM 2250, it was built to work with the company's new 360 series of mainframe computers. Whereas DAC-1 was tailored for the design of automobiles, the 2250 was an easily adaptable general-purpose machine. IBM's commitment gave the nascent field of computer graphics much-needed credibility. One immediate effect was a surge of competition for the business of providing graphics terminals to use with IBM's and other manufacturers' mainframe computers.

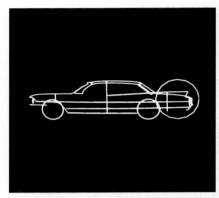

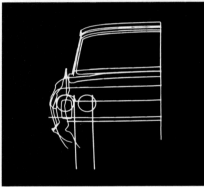

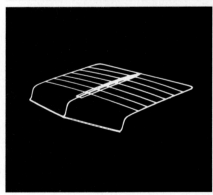

Frames from a 1964 demonstration film show the capabilities of DAC-1, the revolutionary computer-aided design system developed by General Motors and IBM. With the touch of an electronic pencil, the designer of this Cadillac could enlarge a circled area *(top two frames)*, rotate the model *(middle)* or modify the design of the trunk *(bottom)*.

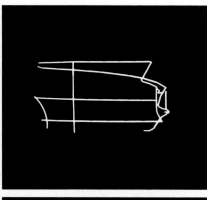

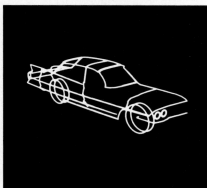

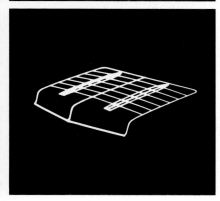

A front runner was Evans & Sutherland Computer Corporation, a Salt Lake City company founded in 1968 by David Evans and Ivan Sutherland. After earning his doctorate from M.I.T., and before joining the faculty of Harvard in 1966, Sutherland had served two years as chief of the information technology program at the Defense Department's Advanced Research Projects Agency (ARPA) at the Pentagon. Evans was doing work for ARPA at the time, and the two formed a vision of what computer graphics could become. Ultimately, Evans & Sutherland would design and sell scientific and engineering workstations and flight simulators for training airline pilots. But one of the first projects the new company tackled was to build a computer graphics terminal that could outperform the IBM 2250.

A QUESTION OF SPEED

Evans & Sutherland took aim at the 2250's major limitation. IBM's system was designed to operate as a terminal relying solely on a graphics program loaded into a mainframe computer. That arrangement, while suitable for tasks that did not require the undivided attention of the computer's central processing unit, limited graphics performance in two ways. First, the software operated too slowly to handle complex drawings such as those for mechanical engineering. In any graphics system, speed is an issue because the computer has to redraw the image continually; if there are more lines on the screen than the computer can redraw in the 1/30 second or so allotted to the task, lines dim and the image flickers. Second, the rotation process took up too much computer time. To rotate a drawing on a terminal screen, the graphics software in the host computer calculated a new position for each line before redrawing it. If the calculations were interrupted, the rotation would become jerky; thus, turning an object around on the screen monopolized the computer, taking precedence over tasks the machine might be asked to perform by other users.

To avoid these two pitfalls, Evans & Sutherland planned to do something radical. The company decided to build special-purpose digital circuits into the terminal of their LDS-1 (for Line Drawing System). These circuits would rotate objects and refresh the screen, thus relieving the host computer and software of those tasks. Evans & Sutherland built a special processor that significantly shortened the time required to refresh the screen, increasing by as much as a factor of 100 the number of lines that could be displayed before flicker set in. This also enabled the machine to change the image on the screen with amazing speed. The LDS-1 astounded Stanley Ruggio, a General Dynamics Corporation engineer who saw it in 1972. "Its speed of putting up the display," he reported, "was awesome—half a second, almost instantaneously."

For all its wizardry, the LDS-1 did not address one issue: the towering cost of computer graphics. It was a bargain, certainly, considering what it could do, but it cost $250,000, twice as much as the IBM 2250. For either machine, the necessary graphics software cost a like amount. In the face of such prices, even large companies that already owned or leased mainframe computers often balked at the cost of adding graphics to the system.

One way to lower the price of a graphics terminal was to curb its voracious appetite for memory in the refresh buffer. For every line in a drawing, the computer had to remember a set of coordinates for each of the two endpoints; for an arc of a circle, three points; and for a free-form curve, hundreds of points. With each point in a three-dimensional image needing eight bytes of storage, the memory requirements for a detailed drawing of an aircraft, say, were astronomical. If these requirements could be reduced or eliminated, a graphics terminal might be built for a fraction of the cost of the Evans & Sutherland device.

As it happened, a device that could break the memory price barrier had been around since 1965, introduced by engineers at an Oregon firm called Tektronix, a builder of oscilloscopes and other electronic test instruments. The direct-view storage tube, or DVST, was much like an ordinary vector graphics CRT, except that it contained a mesh of fine wires behind the phosphor coating on the screen. As the electron beam darted about the screen to draw an image, it charged the wire grid with electricity that kept the image aglow for as long as an hour, making high-priced refresh buffers unnecessary. The cost difference was dramatic. Where a graphics system with a refresh buffer often operated for as much as $250 per hour, a terminal with a direct-view storage tube could operate for $10 to $30 an hour. "The storage tube made graphics affordable for the masses," said Andries van Dam of Brown. "You could hang them as terminals over telephone lines to mainframes and all of a sudden you had el cheapo, poor man's graphics."

There were, to be sure, liabilities, which was why Evans & Sutherland had opted not to use the storage tube in the LDS-1. For one thing, the DVST could produce only two-dimensional images. Furthermore, the image was slow to come up on the screen, and when it did, it was fuzzy; lines were so faint that room lights had to be dimmed for the lines to be visible. More important, selective erasing and rotation were impossible.

Nevertheless, the DVST filled a definite need. Not everyone who could benefit from computer graphics required—or could afford—the sophisticated features of an LDS-1. For example, scientists analyzing graphed data or plotting topographical maps did not need real-time response or the ability to rotate images. Ultimately, Tektronix set the price for DVST terminals at a mere $4,000 each, and thousands of them were sold over the next decade. Until a radical decline in the price of memory made practical a new technological twist, DVSTs would dominate the graphics field.

Techniques
for Revealing
the Invisible

A doctor scrutinizes detailed pictures that expose the body's internal organs without surgery or X-rays. A military reconnaissance satellite scans the earth's surface, pinpointing hostile ships and missile installations. A film technician translates a classic black-and-white movie frame by frame into glowing color. These are vastly different enterprises, but they have in common the technology known as image processing, a versatile array of computing techniques that coax otherwise invisible data out of hiding and display it in a form that yields readily to analysis by machine or study by the human eye.

Image processing can sharpen such familiar pictures as medical X-rays and ordinary photographs. It can also give graphic form to many kinds of data that are not normally perceived as the stuff of images. With the proper software, a computer can generate striking and informative pictures from measurements of radio frequencies, gamma rays, infrared radiation and other phenomena outside the visible spectrum.

Whether an image is intended for interpretation by machine or by the human eye, the first processing step is the translation of the image data into digital form (page 9). The computer divides the image into thousands of points, then assigns a number—a common image processing scale uses the numbers zero through 255—to each point. The numbers can represent radio wavelengths, shades of gray, intensities of heat radiation or any other values chosen by the computer operator. The computer displays the image by using a look-up table—a list of prescribed values—to assign a specific color or brightness to each numbered point, which then appears as a dot on the computer's screen.

Many image processing techniques are simply mathematical manipulations that apply different look-up tables to highlight various kinds of data in an image. For example, a look-up table that distributes colors evenly along a scale of 256 temperature values might depict a flame as a solid mass of hot red against a background of cooler colors. Processed with a look-up table that assigns all its colors to the narrow range of temperatures within the flame, the image would instead reveal the flame's different temperature zones through the entire visible spectrum, from red to violet, and the cooler background would disappear. Similar manipulations can separate closely related values to delineate muscles and organs, distinguish between atmospheric features in a weather system and give easily readable form to many other varieties of data.

A Pair of Versatile Orbiting Scanners

Since 1972, when the first Landsat satellite began peering down from orbit and snapping digital pictures of the earth, thousands of scientists have come to regard Landsat photographs as indispensable research tools. These computer images have helped geologists pinpoint promising sites for oil drilling, enabled ecologists to locate wildlife refuges and water-pollution trouble spots, assisted cartographers in refining their maps of the earth's surface and aided more than 100 nations in shaping their natural resource policies.

The pictures shown here and on the next two pages are computer images generated by *Landsat 4* and *Landsat 5*. These were the first satellites to carry the thematic mapper, or TM, a digital scanner sensitive to wavelengths in seven bands of the electromagnetic spectrum. The TM enabled Landsat to take its first natural color pictures in 1982, using the wavelengths of visible light. The TM can also distinguish between invisible infrared radiation from different species of plants and trees and can create false color pictures—which use arbitrarily assigned colors to differentiate between various surfaces on the basis of heat radiation.

The TM relays data for each of its seven bands to a ground-station computer, where image processing software corrects for angle of sun, time of year and other distorting factors, and then pairs each wavelength band or combination of bands with a color look-up table that converts the digital data into pictures.

Armed with the TM, Landsat orbits 431 miles above the earth, photographing the terrain below in narrow stripes that stretch from pole to pole. Each of these swaths is 115 miles wide; orbiting at the rate of 99 minutes per stripe, the satellite completes a photographic scan of the entire planet once every 16 days.

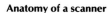

Anatomy of a scanner
The TM employs an intricate arrangement of mirrors and electronic sensors to pick up the seven bands of data used for Landsat's computer images. The scan mirror *(1)* bounces reflected light from the earth's surface past the secondary mirror *(2)* to strike the doughnut-shaped primary mirror *(3)*. Next, the wavelengths reflect back against the secondary mirror and rebound through the hole in the primary mirror to meet the pair of scan-line correction mirrors *(4)*, which realign the reflected wavelengths to compensate for the oscillation of the scan mirror and for Landsat's orbital motion. A silicon detector *(5)* senses three visible wavelengths and one infrared band. The three remaining wavelengths continue on to another doughnut arrangement, consisting of a spherical relay mirror *(6)* and a folding relay mirror *(7)*, which passes the reflection along to detectors *(8 and 9)* that are sensitive to one thermal band and two infrared bands. These detectors are artificially cooled so that they will respond only to reflections from the scan mirror and not to ambient heat from the satellite.

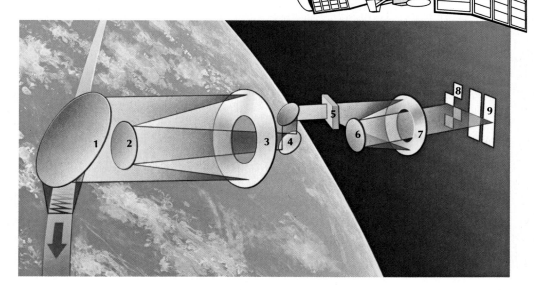

Sharpening Detail by Separating Shades of Gray

One of the most versatile image processing techniques is gray scale transformation, developed to accentuate distinctions between the features in a digital image. Data for digital images usually does not span an entire 256-value gray scale, from black points at zero to white points at 255. If the points of a given image are tightly clustered in a range of grays somewhere between the extremes of that scale, details may blur. To increase the contrast between shades of gray, a look-up table identifies the darkest and lightest values in an image, "stretches" them to black and white respectively, then mathematically distributes intermediate values along the new zero-to-255 continuum. As shades of gray that had nearly identical values in the original image move further apart in the enhanced version, details become easier to distinguish.

Input Data

A1 = Darkest Value Reading
A2 = Any Middle Reading
A3 = Lightest Value Reading

Output Value

0 = Darkest Value
B = Any Middle Value
255 = Lightest Value

$$B = \frac{A_2 - A_1}{A_3 - A_1} \times 255$$

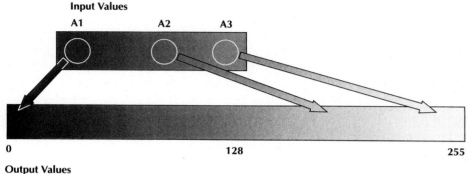

Input Values

A1   A2   A3

0   128   255

Output Values

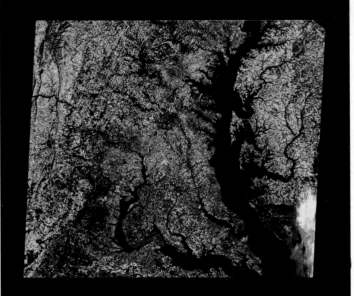

The partially stretched image of the Baltimore/Washington area *(above, left)* and the fully stretched version *(above)* show how contrast enhancing can sharpen and add detail to a Landsat picture. In these false color digital images, red indicates dense vegetation; pinkish gray regions are suburbs; where foliage and buildings are intermingled; built-up urban areas are light blue; and dark blue water shows lighter streaks of pollution.

This false color image of volcanic Mount St. Helens in Washington State *(below)* combines visible-light data from two bands with infrared data from a third. The bright red areas represent woodlands or other dense greenery; light blue areas are sparse vegetation; white areas could be snow, fallow fields, concrete or clouds.

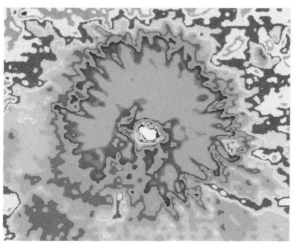

The thematic mapper uses only data from its thermal band to produce this image of the same volcano *(left)*. To highlight temperature variations, the image was contrast-stretched twice. Cold snow is blue in this false color picture; warmer areas are green, and the hottest magma pools are white, surrounded by progressively cooler regions of red, orange and yellow.

This Landsat picture of the mountain *(right)* is in true color, based on data from three bands of the visible spectrum. Dark green areas are forests or other vegetation; white areas indicate snow.

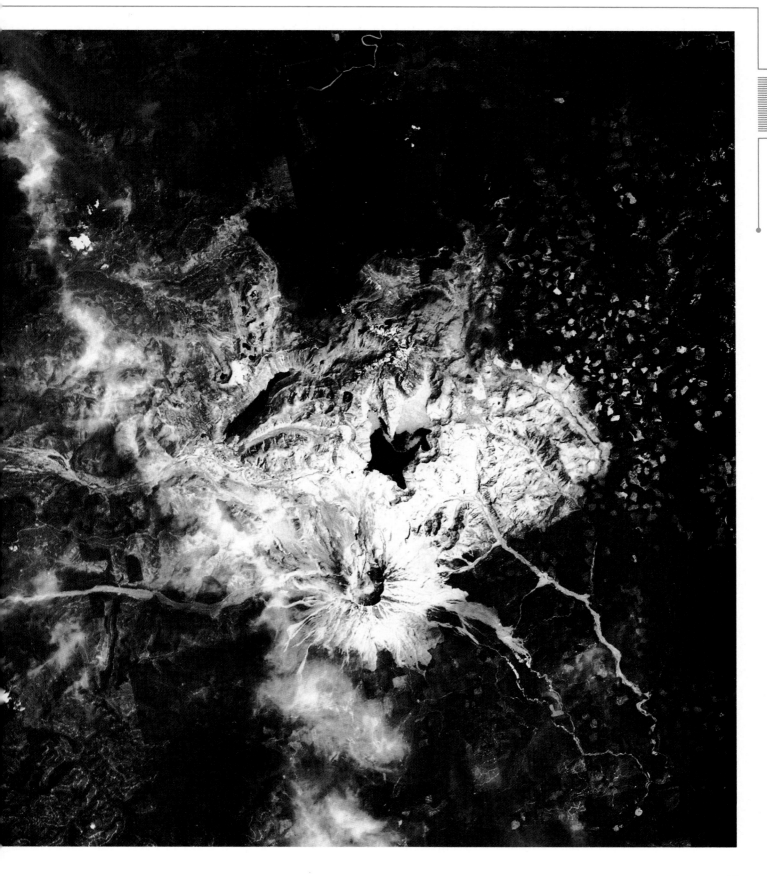

2

Keeping an Eye on the Weather

A Geostationary Operational Environmental Satellite, or GOES, photographs the earth's weather patterns from an orbit more than 22,000 miles high. At that altitude, a GOES circles the earth in 24 hours, the time it takes the planet to rotate once on its axis. This perfect synchronization means that the satellite is always over the same spot, stationary relative to the earth's surface, in a geosynchronous, or geostationary, orbit. A GOES views a much smaller segment of the earth than a Landsat but monitors it 24 hours a day, whereas Landsat sees any given spot only once every 16 days.

Using a visible-infrared spin-scan radiometer, or VISSR, a GOES maps temperature variations on the earth's surface and in the atmosphere. The VISSR uses differences in heat radiation to distinguish between land and water, to locate the boundaries between levels of the atmosphere and to view cloud systems for clues about the behavior of major storms. The satellite's ground-based computer system uses image processing to enhance infrared data, sharpening the contrast between key geographic and meteorological features for better comprehension by the human eye.

Although the GOES system has operated for long periods with only one satellite, it was designed to use two. Dual satellite coverage enables meteorologists to monitor weather patterns over an area extending from western Africa west to New Zealand. The overlap region covered by both satellites encompasses the United States.

Spinning at the rate of 100 rpm, a GOES scans the earth in parallel lines, transmitting each line of digital data to a ground-based computer for image processing. The VISSR use more than 700 lines of data for each digital image of the planet's weather conditions. Another computer transmits sections of the satellite data to television stations and other users around the United States.

Shown as a solid white sphere off the south-eastern coast of the United States, Hurricane Diana swirls across the face of the earth in a standard VISSR infrared image taken in 1984. The unenhanced digital image masks the range of temperature variations inside the storm's canopy of cirrus clouds.

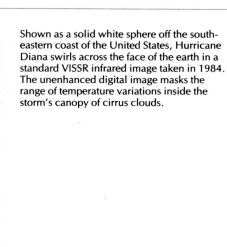

In this view of Diana's internal structure, image processing zooms in on one segment of the VISSR picture, highlighting subtle temperature differences by applying an entire 256-value look-up table to a range of temperatures that spanned only 30 values in the original image. The result is a vivid picture of the storm's temperature zones and precipitation patterns.

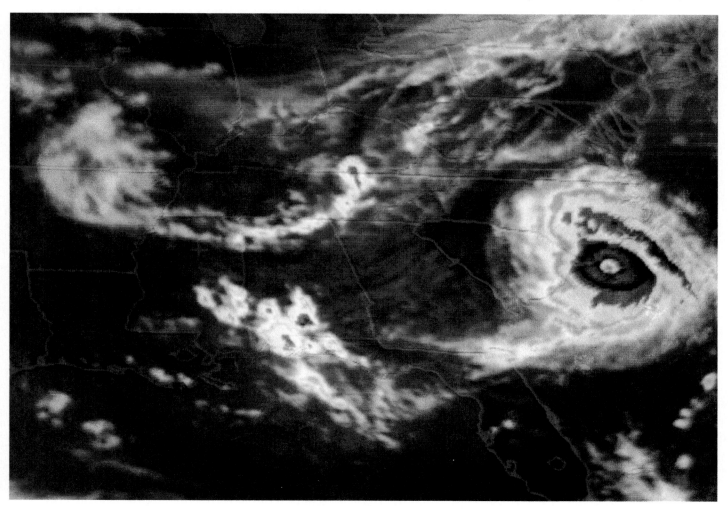

Sophisticated Aids to Diagnosis

Computer imaging is the key to powerful noninvasive techniques for diagnosing the body's internal ills. A positron emission tomography (PET) scanner, for example, takes pictures of internal organs at work by using minute quantities of gamma radiation to track chemical activity inside the body. A nuclear magnetic resonance (NMR) scanner generates its images of the body's interior by using magnetic fields and radio frequencies to manipulate the motion of atomic nuclei in certain elements present in the body.

Unlike X-ray pictures, which use a radiation source outside the body, a PET scan is done by means of internal radiation. Some common biochemical—for example, glucose, in the case of a brain scan—is tagged, or marked, with a short-lived radioactive isotope and injected into the patient. By following the radioactive tag, the PET scanner builds up a picture of where and at what rate the chemical is being absorbed.

An NMR scanner works without introducing any foreign substance into the body. The scanner employs magnetic coils and a radio frequency unit to generate magnetic fields that alter the behavior of atomic nuclei in certain mathematically predictable patterns. By sensing the energy pulses given off by the nuclei as their motion changes, the scanner determines the distribution of various elements within the body. Image processing converts this chemical data into a visual map of organs and tissues.

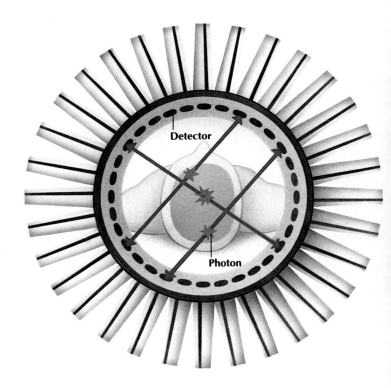

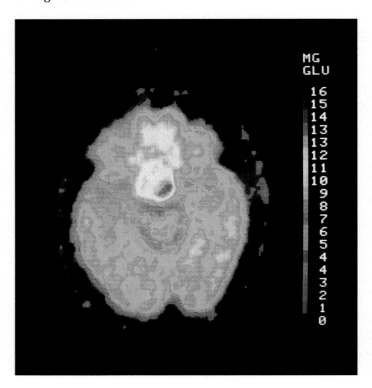

Tracking Glucose in the Brain

A patient's head is ringed by the detectors of the PET scanner (above) as the brain begins to absorb radioactively tagged glucose. Positrons emitted by the tag element collide with nearby electrons, annihilating each other to produce pairs of photons. The photons fly off in opposite directions and impinge on paired detectors. Image processing software uses the photon detection data to locate sites of glucose concentration in the brain, then creates pictures that highlight those sites with variations in brightness or color. Since glucose is a primary source of brain energy, the shifting of glucose absorption patterns reveals changes in brain function. The PET scan image at left shows a reddish orange brain tumor just above the center of the picture. Malignant tumors are readily detected with PET scan technology because they absorb glucose at a significantly higher rate than does normal brain tissue.

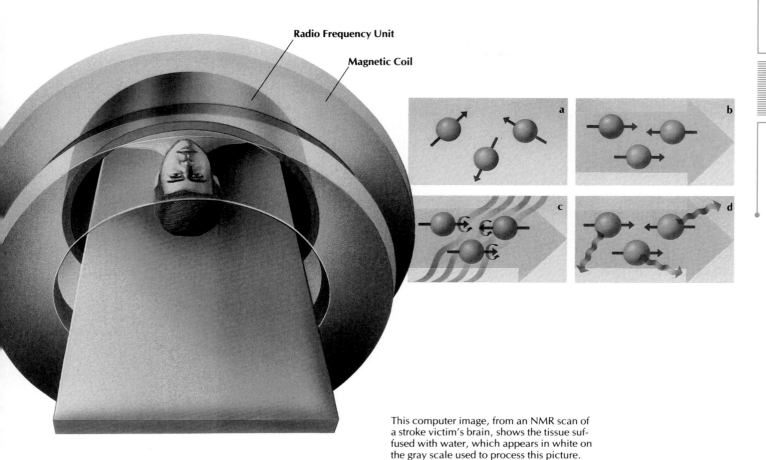

Radio Frequency Unit

Magnetic Coil

This computer image, from an NMR scan of a stroke victim's brain, shows the tissue suffused with water, which appears in white on the gray scale used to process this picture.

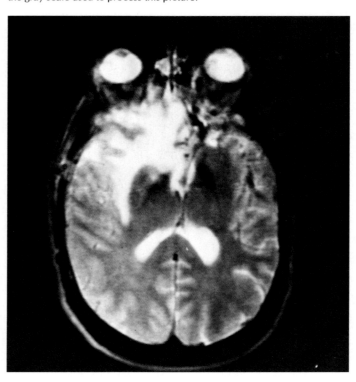

Analyzing Radio Pulses

A patient lies encircled by the thick magnetic coils of an NMR scanner and the flat ring of the scanner's radio frequency unit (above). When the scanner is switched on, a magnetic field realigns some of the body's atomic nuclei (above, right). Each nucleus in its normal state rotates on a randomly oriented axis (a). A magnetic field arranges the nuclei with their axes parallel and lined up either with or against the field (b). The radio frequency unit sets up a second field at right angles to the first, causing the nuclei to wobble as they rotate (c). When the radio frequency unit is turned off, the nuclei relax to their normal rotation (d), giving off radio pulses that are picked up by the scanner.

By applying radio frequency fields of varying wavelengths, and by subjecting the signals from the relaxing nuclei to complex mathematical analysis, the scanner identifies concentrations of a particular element present in the body and assembles a detailed picture of its distribution.

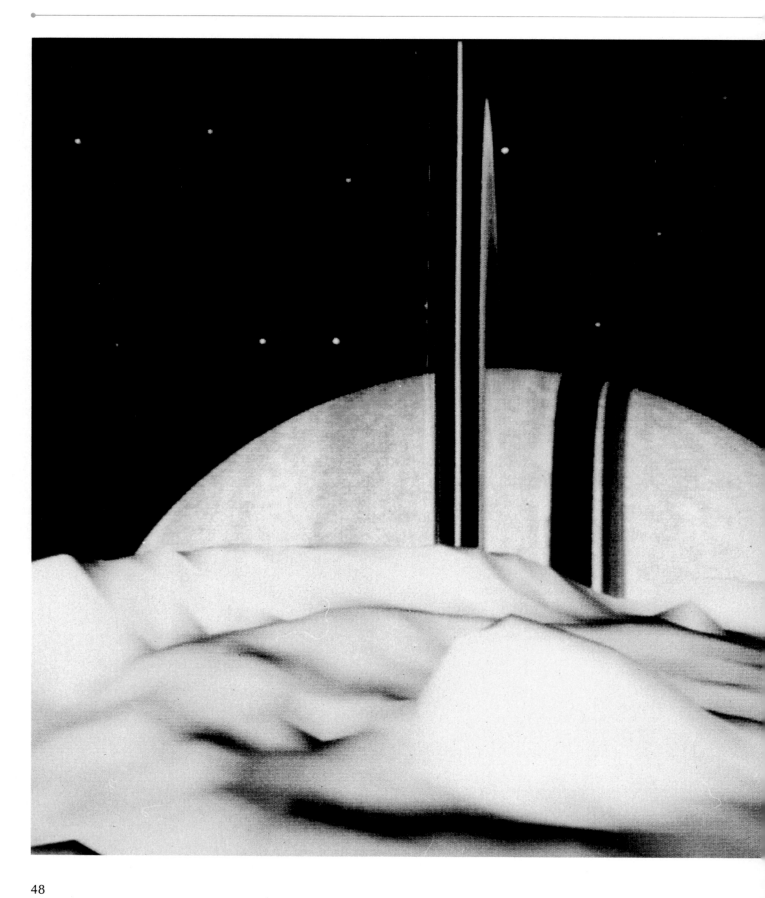

Multiplying the Visual Possibilities

In 1981, at a game arcade near Chicago called One Step Beyond, 15-year-old Steve Juraszek became a local legend and gained some national celebrity by dropping a quarter into the slot of a Defender video game—and spending the next 16 hours and 34 minutes piloting a small spaceship across the video screen before him, using buttons and a joystick to shoot at alien ships and dodge their return fire. At first the pace of the game was not too fast and the movement of the invaders was fairly predictable, but as Juraszek began to pile up points, the action speeded up and the aliens displayed subtler strategies. Soon the screen was a colorful maelstrom of cannon fire, bomb explosions and fast-moving spaceships, pitting Juraszek's reflexes against a small special-purpose computer inside the game console. The computer drew continuously changing images on the screen that reflected both the player's actions and the responses generated by the machine's game program. And when the tiring Juraszek's last ship was blasted to bits, ending the marathon game, the computer was ready to start over.

Most players, less skillful or lucky than Juraszek, got only a few minutes of play for each coin they put into video games like Defender, but their persistence (in some cases almost to the point of addiction) helped fuel a video game craze that swept much of the industrialized world in the late 1970s and early 1980s. Thousands upon thousands of machines appeared in arcades, pizza parlors and shopping malls; almost overnight, millions of home video games were sold as well. Few players realized, or would even have cared, how the machines worked; what made the games fascinating was their rapid response to everything the player did, and the complexity and realism of the images on the screen, which seemed to increase with each new game. In fact, these video games were sophisticated, if highly specialized, interactive computer graphics systems; for millions of players, a video game provided the first hands-on experience with a computer.

Bathed in brilliant sunlight, the planet Saturn is seen as if from the surface of its moon Mimas. This computer image was produced at California's Jet Propulsion Laboratory from data beamed back to earth by the Voyager spacecraft and combined with a graphics program by Dr. James Blinn. Such complex pictures became possible when increased computer memory was allied with raster graphics techniques.

This democratization of computer graphics was made possible by a familiar technology that had long been too expensive for any application without a sky-high budget. This was raster graphics, a system that uses a video screen, like that of an ordinary television set, divided into phosphorescent picture elements, or pixels, arranged in hundreds of horizontal lines *(page 22)*. The color and brightness of the pixels are regulated by the intensity of the electron beams that scan the screen from top to bottom, refreshing the image at least 30 times per second. The lighting information for the image is stored in the system's frame buffer, an electronic list in the computer's memory that specifies the intensity of each pixel.

Although a raster monitor can display images of far greater realism than the line drawings produced on a vector monitor, the memory requirements of raster systems made them prohibitively expensive for many years. A raster frame buffer must hold lighting information for every pixel on the screen *(page 52)*, not just for the coordinates of the key points of lines or curves, as in the case of vector systems. Since the screen of an average home television set may have close to 250,000 pixels, clearly even the most basic raster system requires a huge memory base for its frame buffer, particularly if color is added.

Until the 1960s, the predominant computer memory technology was costly magnetic core storage. Developed in the early 1950s to replace the slow and unreliable vacuum-tube memories of first-generation computers, magnetic core memories consisted of iron rings strung like beads on a wire grid. Each ring could be magnetized and, depending on the magnetic polarity applied to it, could store a binary one or zero; the memory's contents could be updated quickly and easily by changing the polarity. Magnetic core memories were used with early vector graphics systems linked to large mainframes, but at a typical price of $500,000 per million bits—enough for just four frames of black-and-white TV—they were out of reach for the hefty memory requirements of all but a few raster systems.

A cheaper alternative to the magnetic core was a rotating "drum" memory, used on the earliest raster frame buffers in the mid-1960s. This was a large cylinder that worked like a magnetic audio or video tape, storing bits of data corresponding to pixel intensities. A series of tracks ran in parallel bands around a drum. Each track carried a string of bits, with each bit corresponding to a single pixel in a line of pixels on the screen. As the drum rotated, the value for each pixel was read and converted to control signals for the electron beams of the video tube; one rotation of the drum completely refreshed a row of pixels. A drum cost nearly $30,000 and could store data for about 10 frames of pictures.

Since memory was so expensive, raster technology was employed only where its advantages were critical. As early as the mid-1960s, for example, raster monitors were used in electric power companies, subway system control centers and scientific labs, where color displays were a key to monitoring activities.

One early user of large-scale raster graphics was the National Aeronautics and Space Administration. NASA's first interplanetary probes used systems like those employed in commercial television to send back pictures from space, but in 1968 NASA launched *Mariner 6*, the first spacecraft to use a computerized raster-scan device. As *Mariner 6* neared Mars, in 1969, its scanning light sensors recorded the planet's features in digital form; this data was beamed back to earthbound antennas, then fed to an IBM computer, which processed the images for display on a modified television set. The few hundred pictures, showing craters and

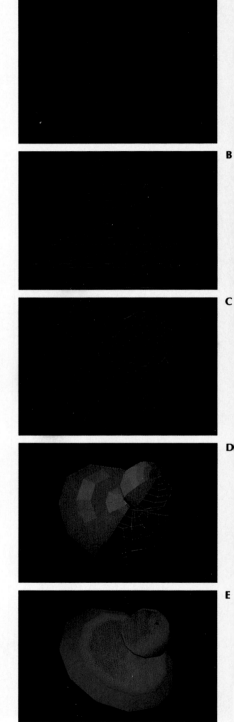

Evolution of an Image
To create a realistic 3-D image, a computer artist begins with an outline called a spine (A) to mark the outer dimensions of the object. Repeated across 360 degrees, the spine forms a solid made up of multiple polygons joined at the edges (B); specifying movement along two axes causes the solid to tilt (C). The artist selects colors and a light source, then runs a flat shading program to fill in surfaces (D). For the final image (E), a technique called Phong shading (for Bui Tuong Phong, the University of Utah programmer who devised it) mathematically smooths out the edges between polygons.

channels that looked like dry riverbeds, whetted the appetites of space researchers; by 1972, *Mariner 9* was providing a virtual feast of computerized images showing huge volcanoes, vast canyons, sandy deserts and icecaps at both poles.

Yet even NASA sometimes had to accept cheaper substitutes for raster graphics. In the late 1960s, the agency had bought several flight simulators for training Apollo astronauts to land on the moon. Each simulator incorporated video screens in a full-scale model of the lunar lander, but the pictures displayed on the screens were not computer graphics. Instead, the images were produced by a TV camera pointed at a miniature model of the moon's surface; the camera was controlled by a computer linked to the controls of the simulator. This roundabout system provided real-time responses with much less demand for computer memory than would have been required by a full-fledged raster graphics setup. NASA used a similar system to train early test crews for the space shuttle; not until the late 1970s were computer graphics fully integrated into the shuttle simulators.

POWERHOUSE ON A SILICON CHIP

The evolution of graphics technology from custom-made, multimillion-dollar systems to ubiquitous video games was brought about by technical advances that made computers faster and memory cheaper. The process began in the early 1970s, with the introduction of "shift-register" frame buffers using integrated circuits, or ICs. An IC is a single small chip of silicon that contains a number of electronic components; because of its compactness, an IC operates much faster than the same combination of independent parts wired together.

An IC can be used either to process or to store binary information. In the shift-register frame buffer of a raster graphics system, hundreds of ICs record the lighting information for all the pixels on the screen, one or more ICs for each row of pixels, depending on the system. A shift-register frame buffer works on the same principle as the rotating drum, circulating bit by bit through a refresh cycle. Each time an electrical pulse is applied to an IC, an information bit is displaced at one end of the register and its intensity value is read. The bit is then electronically reinserted at the other end of the register, with all the other bits shifting one place. One complete circulation of bits represents the refresh cycle of a single scan line.

Because they were electronic rather than mechanical, shift-register frame buffers were faster than rotating drums. Both types, however, often suffered from a problem called latency, manifested as a delay of several seconds between the user's input and the resulting change on the screen. The problem arose because the intensity of a pixel could be changed only when the bit holding its value came around again in the refresh cycle; before the image on the screen could be replaced, the entire sequence of values for the new image had to be completed, a process made lengthier when many pixels were used to produce complex images. While shift-register systems could produce highly realistic pictures, latency problems made them impractical for interactive situations where speed was important. A flight simulator for training a jet pilot, for example, is useless if the picture before the pilot's eyes does not evolve instantaneously.

The real breakthrough in raster graphics came with the commercial introduction, in the early 1970s, of affordable and powerful random-access memory (RAM) chips. Whereas the first IC memory chips used in shift-register frame buffers stored data sequentially, so that it was available only once in each cycle,

Resolution Enough to Fool the Eye

A computer requires a vast amount of memory to produce an image that can satisfy the remarkable acuity of the human eye. A person with 20/20 vision can detect, on a white background held at reading distance, a black dot ³⁄₁,₀₀₀ of an inch wide. Color resolution is equally amazing. Any hue can be described by the wavelength of light it reflects measured in Angstrom units, about four billionths of an inch. Someone who is not color-blind can perceive a difference between two abutting bands of color that differ in wavelength by as little as 10 Angstrom units.

As illustrated at right, fine dot resolution is useless without good color resolution, and vice versa. In the most demanding circumstances—projection in a movie theater, for example—a computer needs something on the order of 24-million-pixel resolution to rid an image of a mosaic look. And to ensure that there is a continuous gradation of tone from the highlights of an object to the shadows demands a palette of nearly 17 million colors.

The requisite number of hues can be mixed from the additive primary colors—red, blue and green—if there are 256 densities of each. As shown below, each additional bit of memory assigned to manage color doubles the number of densities available. Only eight bits need be assigned to each primary color to achieve the necessary range of tones. But each pixel on the screen requires 24 bits of memory—eight for each additive primary tone—to register the color assigned to it. Thus a 24-million-pixel screen must be backed by nearly 576 million bits of computer memory.

1 BIT

2 BITS

3 BITS

4 BITS

MEMORY AND COLOR
Adding another bit of computer memory to the number of bits used to describe a color doubles the number of tones that can be displayed. With a single bit *(top left)*, only two choices are possible: A given color is either on or off. A pair of bits can be turned on or off in four ways—both bits on, both off, and two combinations of one on and one off—and each bit can be assigned to a different color intensity. Three bits offer eight shades, four bits 16 shades and so on.

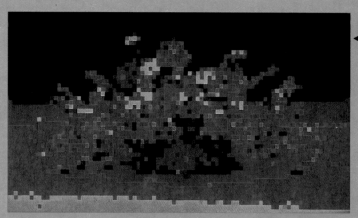

MAKINGS OF A NATURAL IMAGE

◄ The high-contrast, stair-step image at left simulates the best result that a computer graphics system having low-color and low-pixel resolution could produce. Color resolution is limited to a single bit of memory assigned to each of the primary colors, red, blue and green, allowing them to be turned either on or off *(black)*. Further degraded by the small number of pixels available—only 30,000 for this example—the picture is barely recognizable as a cheerful arrangement of cut flowers.

3

Adding lifelike color without improving the ► system's pixel resolution brightens the image but makes it no more convincing than the one produced by low-resolution color. Indeed, the full range of colors only emphasizes the mosaic-like structure camouflaged to a large degree in the picture above by the small number of colors available.

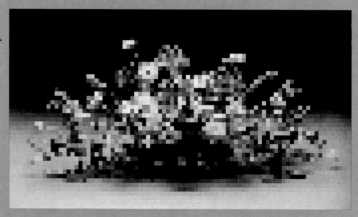

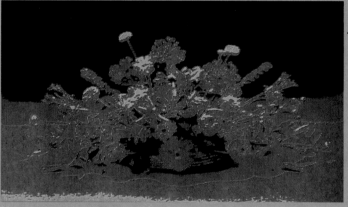

◄ High-resolution pixels combined with a limited selection of colors yield an image that is no more realistic than either of the preceding ones. Tiny pixels—263,000 in this picture—reduce the stepped appearance of the flowers, but the presence of only three colors robs the scene of any realism.

A computer graphics system that combines ► good color resolution with high-resolution pixels produces an image that has the realism of a photograph. Because of the small scale of reproduction, this picture required only 4,096 colors and slightly more than one million bits of computer memory.

RAM chips are designed so that any bit of information can be recalled by the computer's central processor at any time. In a RAM-based raster graphics system, a specific memory location is designated to hold the intensity value for each pixel. This array of electronic pigeonholes is called a bit map; its contents change constantly as it receives fresh input from the user or from the program controlling the computer. A device called a display controller converts the information in the bit map into instructions for the scanning beam of the video display. Because the computer can update the bit map even while the display controller is refreshing the screen, any delay between a user's input and the corresponding change on the screen is virtually imperceptible. A RAM-based system is thus far less susceptible to the latency problem common to drum and shift-register buffers.

In 1968, the most advanced RAM chips could store 256 bits each and cost more than one dollar per bit. Considering that nearly 1,000 such chips would be needed to store the pixel information necessary to produce a single image on a medium-resolution monochrome monitor, RAM chips were not cheap. Indeed, they were about twice as expensive as the equivalent in magnetic core memory. But by late 1970, manufacturing advances had made a 1,024-bit chip available; moreover, this 1K (for one-kilobit, or one-thousand-bit) RAM chip was economically competitive with other types of memory.

Fueled by voracious demand for computer memory—partly generated by the boom in computer games—the RAM chip industry took off. Over the next 15 years, it raced past a succession of milestones: 4K (1973), 16K (1975), 64K (1980), 256K (1983) and an awesome one million K RAM (1984). The cost per bit of memory went down as chip capacity rose; as computer consultant Carl Machover noted, "If the price of cars had gone down like the price of memory, I could get a Rolls-Royce for a dollar." With the advent of powerful and inexpensive RAM chips, raster systems were no longer limited by the cost of memory; by the mid-1970s, the appearance of other technical advances had helped open the way for the use of raster graphics in a variety of areas.

REALISM VERSUS SPEED

Though the demands placed on raster graphics systems change from one application to another, two desirable properties—speed and resolution—always operate at cross purposes. That is, the more realistic the image desired, the higher the resolution and the more varied the color palette must be. But this means that at any given moment, the memory must hold a huge amount of information about the image, and any change to the image places a great burden on the computer. Unless it has a fast and powerful processor, the system is forced to slow down. Designers of both hardware and software for computer graphics have therefore worked not only to find shortcuts that reduce the amount of memory required for complex images but to develop new ways of rapidly processing image data.

A major advance came in 1974 during work on a project to produce computer-enhanced images, using data from satellites that monitored earth resources such as farmlands, forests and mineral deposits. Since myriad colors would be needed to depict the many variables recorded by the satellites, project designers set out to develop a system with a massive memory base. The breakthrough occurred when the designers realized that they could cut memory requirements dramatically by using only a few hundred colors for any single image: The palette for each image

Smoothing Rough Edges

Curved and diagonal edges on a raster display often show a jagged effect known as aliasing. But in the image at right, the edges have been smoothed out with a technique called antialiasing.

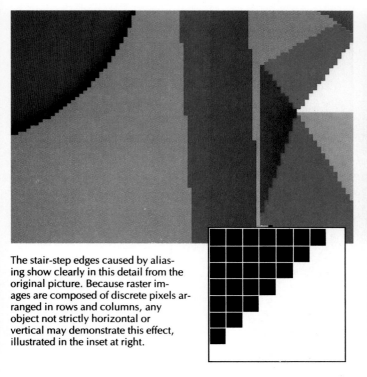

The stair-step edges caused by aliasing show clearly in this detail from the original picture. Because raster images are composed of discrete pixels arranged in rows and columns, any object not strictly horizontal or vertical may demonstrate this effect, illustrated in the inset at right.

In the same detail after antialiasing, pixels adjoining the objects' edges have been assigned a color value midway between that of the object and its background, as shown in this inset. The result is a blurring that reduces contrast and produces a smoother contour.

Altering Images in the Machine

In the real world, the Statue of Liberty stands on an island in New York Harbor, while the Eiffel Tower looms over Paris, near the banks of the River Seine. In the more flexible realm of computerized image processing, however, both of these landmarks can be convincingly transplanted to flank the United Nations Building, against a Manhattan skyline that has been impishly altered in other ways as well *(opposite, below)*.

Such computer-generated prestidigitation has dramatically changed the art of photographic reproduction. For just as word-processing systems juggle words, sentences and para-

To generate an altered view of Manhattan, the image-processing technician scans an actual cityscape *(above)* into the computer and does the same with a photograph of the Statue of Liberty *(far left)*. The statue's computer image is then moved adjacent to the spot selected for its relocation and reduced to its proper relative size *(left)*.

graphs, image processors can manipulate the myriad pixels on a computer screen and alter the colors, textures, sizes and positions of objects. Gone are conventional and time-consuming retouching and darkroom techniques: The results of each change are visible almost immediately.

Advertisers resort to image processing to enhance the appearance of their goods; publications use the new technology to improve the quality and composition of their illustrations. In the early 1980s, for example, *National Geographic* magazine shifted an Egyptian pyramid to make it fit more readily in a cover photograph, and *The New York Times Magazine* ran a picture in which an empty space in the landscape had been enhanced with fake shrubbery.

Some defend such practices as matters of editorial discretion, but others point to the dangers of a technology that can so deftly manipulate the content of photographs. As one graphics consultant has warned, the computerized retouching of supposedly documentary images is "one of the few areas in which one can do true counterfeiting and not have it be observed."

The image of the statue is copied pixel by pixel and placed on its new midtown site *(left)*. In the finished overall view below *(reading clockwise from left center)*, a series of similar operations has produced a version of Manhattan that includes—among other alterations—the Eiffel Tower, a slightly taller and relocated Empire State Building, the Chrysler tower replaced by San Francisco's Transamerica pyramid, a skewed Citicorp Building and an additional pier.

could be chosen by the user, or by the program, from a stored list of thousands, even millions, of options. This insight led to the development of the so-called color look-up table, a system quickly adopted for many graphics applications.

The key principle of the look-up table is that the frame buffer does not store explicit color information for each pixel but instead merely points to the addresses in memory where that information is stored. For example, a frame buffer using eight bits to describe each pixel can produce only 256 combinations of the red, blue and green beams that create color images on a screen. But if those eight bits were used to choose from 256 addresses, the colors stored at those addresses could be chosen in turn from a virtually limitless range of hue, intensity and saturation. (In a system using 32 bits to describe each pixel, there are more than 4.3 billion choices.) Furthermore, a given system's look-up table can be reprogrammed for particular types of images. Where blues and greens predominate, for instance, the table might include only a few shades of red; if the image is to be very dark, the selection would omit the lightest tones. Yet even a limited palette for each image can provide smooth shading and subtle distinctions of tone.

The ability to create many intensities of a single color helps overcome a characteristic of raster systems—known as the jaggies—that detracts from image realism. Because of the gridlike layout of pixels on a raster screen, a horizontal or vertical line will appear smooth and straight, but a diagonal line will have a jagged, or stepped, profile, like a staircase made of square blocks. This problem, also called aliasing (from the mathematical function that describes it), can be minimized by using a screen with higher resolution; like the edge of an Egyptian pyramid seen from afar, a jagged line of very tiny pixels will appear smooth compared with a line made up of larger pixels. But high-resolution screens require proportionately more memory; another solution is to use variable intensities to build antialiasing features into the graphics software *(page 55)*.

Although the availability of large blocks of memory for frame buffers made raster graphics feasible in the first place, it also created new problems in processing the resulting huge volume of data. Most computers are built according to the architectural principles of computer pioneer John von Neumann, who determined that machines should work on each task serially, or one step at a time, with the central processing unit, or CPU, directing the movement of information as well as performing all computations. Inherent in this design is the possibility of a so-called von Neumann bottleneck, which can occur whenever a processor has to spend so much time directing the flow of information to and from memory that its data-processing speed is reduced.

To help break the bottleneck, system designers began turning to special hardware that would work in parallel with the CPU. Some chips, called coprocessors, are specialized versions of the chips used for CPUs; they provide high-speed assistance just for crunching numbers. Other chips perform some of the special functions required by especially graphics-intensive applications such as flight simulation, computer-aided design and film making. (Indeed, the rapid decline in the cost of ICs has been at least partly due to the use of computer-aided design in the making of the chips themselves.)

At root, graphic functions are mathematical, and developing them requires a mixture of creativity and dogged attention to the numbers involved in manipulating images. Notes Dr. James Blinn, a computer scientist who since 1978 has been

Though they look vastly different, these two surreal landscapes are identical in their geometry and were created by the same software. The top picture, however, was produced with instructions that specified an even light to be reflected from all surfaces; the bottom image was created with instructions that specified a distinct light source, thus producing shadows.

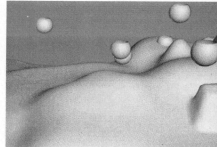

simulating flybys of Jupiter, Saturn and other planets: "Artists make pictures by putting paint on canvas. Computer graphics people make pictures by inventing mathematical functions that, when plotted, look like things." But if scientists such as Blinn are at home with the mathematical origins of computer graphics, most users would prefer to create and transform images without having to handle algebra or trigonometry.

To make computer graphics accessible to these users, the mathematical functions must be encoded in software; a whole set of complicated instructions for the computer can then be set in motion by a few simple commands. Ivan Sutherland's Sketchpad was the first such software; during the 1960s and 1970s, increasingly complex techniques such as ray tracing and texture mapping *(pages 61-73)* were developed to improve computer graphics' realism. These new techniques began to be applied to a variety of jobs ranging from industrial design to chemical research, triggering an even greater demand for sophisticated graphics systems. In a cycle that came to be known as the silicon treadmill, manufacturers found that they could sell enough of their systems to justify the expense of incorporating graphics software into specialized microchips that in turn could simplify and speed up the systems themselves. By the mid-1980s, even low-cost home computers were equipped with chips containing basic graphics functions.

Throughout the 1970s and early 1980s, computer graphics became more and more common as part of the world's visual landscape. Television networks routinely used computers to make colorful, rapidly changing images to promote their programs. Film producers went further, inserting sequences of computer-generated special effects into movies that took viewers to such inaccessible destinations as deep space or the inside of a computer game. And game designers introduced millions of people to a host of interactive graphics possibilities, from electronic ping-pong tables to road-racing courses. But during this same period,

The program that produced the flasks at right stipulated that they be identical in shape and face the same two simultaneous light sources—a distant one, such as the sun, and one nearby, such as a light bulb. The programmer then called for each flask to be made of a different material or finished in a subtly different color. The program generated shading and highlights based on formulas that specify how light reflects from various surfaces.

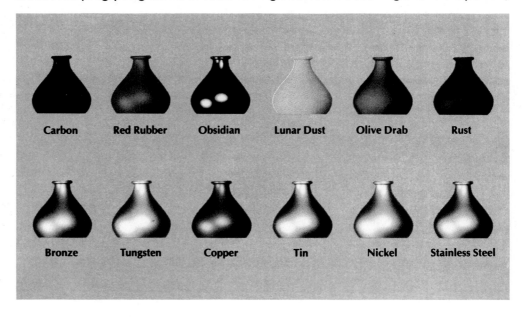

Carbon Red Rubber Obsidian Lunar Dust Olive Drab Rust

Bronze Tungsten Copper Tin Nickel Stainless Steel

graphics were becoming more than an end product. Some computer scientists realized that the immediacy of graphics, which allowed game players to interact almost intuitively with special-purpose computers, could be used to help make computers easier for novices to operate.

AN EXPERIMENT IN PERSONAL COMPUTING

The idea of human-computer communication—the user interface, as it is called—based on visual symbols rather than cryptic words or long strings of numbers found physical expression as early as 1973 in an experimental computer called Alto. Developed at Xerox Corporation's Palo Alto Research Center (PARC), Alto provided individual users with features previously available only in larger, shared systems. These included a big RAM memory (64K, expandable to 256K), a central processor that could gobble six million instructions per second, bit-mapped raster graphics and a mouse *(page 20)* for positioning the cursor, or pointer, on the screen. But one of Alto's most revolutionary features was its graphics-based user interface, which made interaction with the computer similar to a game. The user manipulated the mouse so that the cursor pointed to an icon—a picture on the screen symbolizing a particular function, such as starting a program. When the user pressed a button on the mouse, the function would begin—all without the user having to remember or type a single command.

Alto's bit-mapped frame buffer also made possible a new way of displaying text on the screen. Computers without bit maps could display only one document or image at a time. Alto could display a document, then change the contents of just part of the frame buffer to display another document—or a picture—on a segment of the screen. In effect, Alto's screen became an electronic desktop, where several related files could be shuffled, combined and recombined by manipulating the mouse and selecting icons for various procedures. The Xerox researchers found that first-time computer users quickly picked up the basics and were able to begin doing productive work without lengthy training.

Xerox built 2,000 Alto computers for use within the company but did not immediately try to market the new technology. The ideas behind the computer, however, were seized upon by other companies. And rather than guarding its breakthroughs from competitors, PARC eventually shared many of them with the rest of the world. In 1979, for example, engineers from Apple Computer, founded just three years earlier, were briefed at PARC on the graphics and other concepts pioneered by Alto. Instant converts, they returned to Apple and launched the research and development that led four years later to the introduction of Lisa and then Macintosh, personal computers whose graphics-based software set new standards for user friendliness. Other manufacturers soon began to incorporate newly developed graphics hardware into low-cost systems and to develop software that incorporated some of the Alto's features. By the mid-1980s, graphics capability had become a major selling point for mass-marketed personal computers, with increasing emphasis on graphics-based user interfaces.

With the advent of these personal computers, graphics for everyday use had at last arrived. Graphics pioneer Andries van Dam, commenting on the explosion of graphics features in even the simplest home computers, saw the start of a new era. "Schoolchildren will grow up never realizing that graphics is something special," he noted, adding, "a computer can no longer afford not to speak graphics."

The Secrets of Creating a Realistic Image

By 1950, computer scientists working in graphics could produce, on a computer screen, a moving blip that simulated a bouncing ball. But with the increases in computer memory and speed achieved since then, graphics programmers have raised their visualizing standards vastly higher. Today, they seek nothing less than photographic realism, not just for static images but for animated ones as well. Furthermore, they want their systems to be accessible to any beginner sitting at a simple computer.

To achieve these aims, programmers are working to improve the two fundamentals of creating a computer graphic—modeling and rendering. In modeling, an artist or a designer builds, in effect, a mathematical model of the image by introducing all the structural information, such as which points are to be joined by lines or curves, or where a sphere attaches to a cube. Abstract information—how a scene might change in response to different lighting, for example—must also be declared. In rendering, an operator instructs the computer to display the model's final colors, textures, highlights and shadows on the screen.

Sophisticated graphics systems usually combine both kinds of programs. Some, such as the solid-modeling software explained on pages 62-63 and the paint system shown on pages 72-73, allow the user to work interactively—that is, to construct a model, then modify, color and shade it and watch the results appear instantly on the screen. Other systems accept instructions only in the form of a typed program, requiring hours or days of calculation before producing a display. With advances in computer technology, however, even these programs may become interactive. And if the supercomputers of the 1980s become the desktop computers of the future, spectacular versions of all these methods may be available to anyone who wishes to use them. Until then, the systems showcased on the following pages are "high-end" commercial technology, employed primarily by film makers, advertisers and big manufacturers.

This caterpillar, featured in the video game Worm War I, was constructed with a solid-modeling program and consists entirely of spheres and ellipsoids. The creature's head is a sphere tacked to a chain of spherical body segments, which appear flattened because they overlap. Single ellipsoids, banded with red and yellow, form the caterpillar's eyes and legs.

Complex Solids from a Handful of Building Blocks

To draw a cube, schoolchildren overlap two squares, join the corners with parallel lines and then erase the edges of the cube that the front surfaces would conceal. Wire-frame computer drawing programs *(page 30)* mimic this awkward approach to making solid shapes.

Solid-modeling systems are a substantial improvement. In addition to defining the edges of an object, such programs define the object's surfaces. Boundary representation systems are one way of accomplishing this. In essence, they are wire-frame drawing programs with the added features of surface recognition and the ability to automatically remove hidden lines, such as the ones that form the rear corner of a cube.

Another method, constructive solid geometry (CSG), works according to a different principle. CSG systems come equipped with a selection of three-dimensional building blocks called primitives *(below)*. Using primitives to construct an object such as the caterpillar at left is more like sculpture than drawing. A designer can add one shape to another, building, for example, an ice-cream cone out of an inverted cone and a sphere. With different instructions, an artist can subtract shapes (a block with a round hole in it is a rectangular solid minus a cylinder) or use one primitive as a pattern for another one. The final step is to color the object, shading tones to emphasize its three-dimensionality.

These shapes are representative of the building-block primitives available to an artist using a CSG modeling program. Some, including the doughnut-like toroid floating above the others, are common geometric shapes. Others, such as the four-mounded object and cloverleaf on the right and the oddly bust-shaped figure on the left, are special-purpose primitives invented by the graphics expert who programmed the system.

Particle systems within a particle system generated this planet-engulfing inferno for the movie Star Trek II. As shown in the diagram at left, an "explosion" system positioned particles randomly along rings centered at the outbreak of the fire. Each of the particles forming the innermost ring set off a secondary explosion that sprayed out random particles to create a wall of fire that advanced ring by ring.

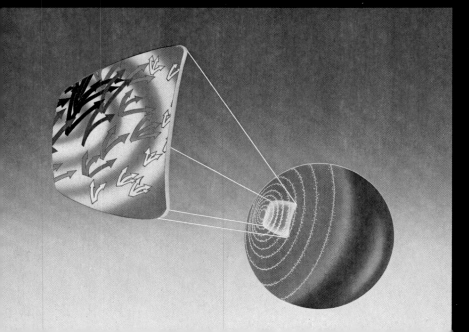

The clumps of grass growing among th beach flora at right were created by an ex plosive particle system similar to the on that produced the conflagration above. Fo a blade of grass, the complete path o each particle is displayed; for a flame, only streak appears. A similar technique drev the other plants in the picture. Like a parti cle system, it employs a randomizing fac

Systems That Mimic Nature

Imitating the random quality of nature—dancing flames, irregularly branching trees, faults and fissures in mountains—is beyond the capabilities of solid-modeling programs. Drawing each limb of an oak or every crack in a cliff would require too much of an artist's—and a computer's—time. Moreover, the hard-edged outlines that these programs produce are ill-suited to flames and other "fuzzy" objects such as clouds or grass.

Procedural modeling techniques are able to surmount these difficulties. Programs for drawing trees or fire, each imbued with a degree of randomness, are loaded into the computer. The artist then indicates a starting point to the machine; electronics does the rest.

One variety of procedural modeling, called a particle system, excels at creating images of fuzzy objects. As the diagram on the opposite page illustrates, a particle system builds a picture by recording the paths of thousands of tiny points of light. Written into the system's program are restrictions on speed, brightness, reaction to gravity and other factors governing the motion of each particle. The result can be as spectacular as the advancing conflagration at left or as subtle as the still life below.

The World's Irregular Geometry

Drawing a credible landscape with a computer was once an onerous undertaking. An artist might spend hours at the keyboard combining straight lines, curves, cones and pyramids, and still not create a realistic scene. But since 1975, the task has greatly eased, thanks to French mathematician Dr. Benoit Mandelbrot. Research he did over a period of more than two decades led to techniques that allow computers to build images of landscapes and other natural forms that look like the real thing—as well as shapes that do not quite resemble anything on earth.

Mandelbrot named the result of his research fractal geometry, for the fractional dimension of certain geometrical forms. For instance, a line is one-dimensional; a plane is two-dimensional; but a curving line that covers almost all of the points on a plane can be said to have a dimension somewhere between one and two. According to Mandelbrot, fractals "tackle the chancy intricacies of nature—bark patterns on oak trees, mud cracks in a dry riverbed, the profile of a broccoli spear. They are a family of irregular shapes with just enough regularity so that they can be mathematically described."

The simplest fractal-generating procedures are little more than rules for replication of a basic shape, which may repeat itself hundreds or thousands of times on an ever-changing scale. A degree of randomness introduced into such formulas makes the results somewhat unpredictable and can lead to a convincingly natural appearance *(right)* or to geometrical shapes of intriguing complexity *(below)*.

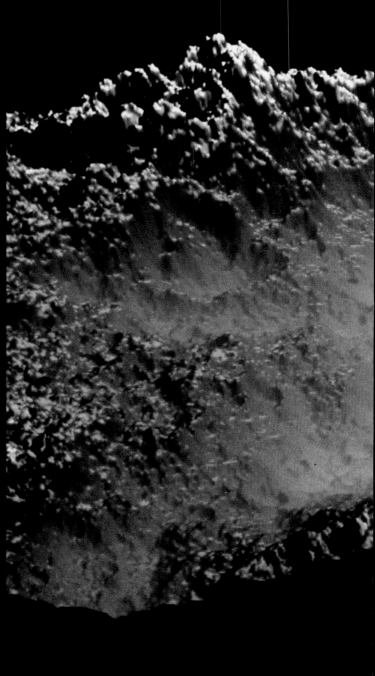

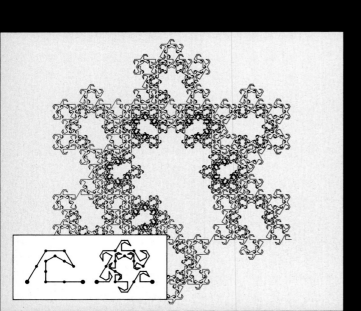

To create the snowflake-like construction at left, a fractal procedure replaced each of the 11 segments of the hook-shaped line in the inset with the entire shape, hundreds of times. When necessary, the formula shrank the hook to prevent it from overlapping its predecessors, leading to a convoluted maze with an intricacy constrained only by the limits of the display's resolution.

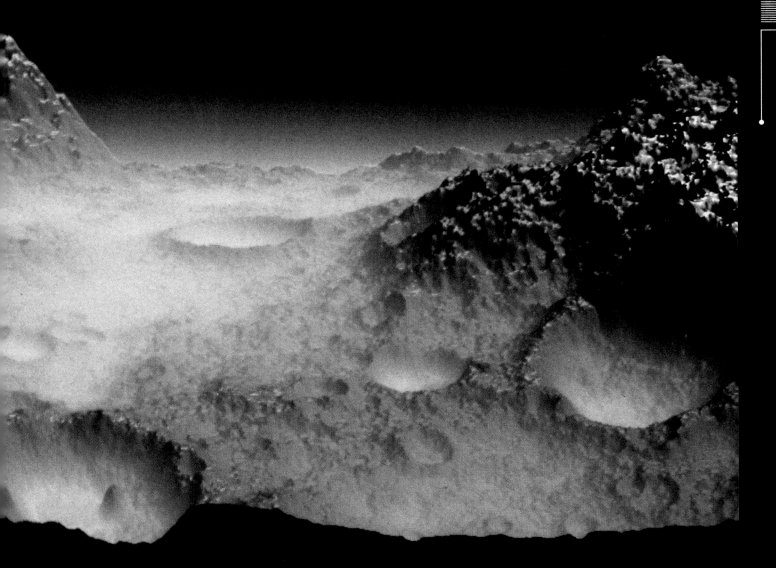

This fractal mountain range was produced
by a chain of repetitive calculations similar
in principle to the one that generated the
pattern at left. However, a randomness factor introduced into the process resulted
in a convincingly rugged landscape instead
of a design of geometric regularity.

Tracing the Path of a Ray of Light

To mimic reality, computer graphics must imitate the intricate play of light in a scene, where countless individual rays are reflected from shiny surfaces, absorbed by dull ones, blocked by opaque objects and transmitted, to a greater or lesser degree, by transparent and translucent ones. For a computer to emulate these effects requires a rendering technique called ray tracing.

The procedure evolved from software designed to determine how nuclear radiation would pass through or around solid objects; the program traced the progress of a ray from the end of its path back to its source. The developers realized that the same process could apply to light rays in images generated by computer. An operator first describes the scene to the computer, including the shape, position, colors and textures of each object as well as the positions, colors and intensities of the light sources illuminating it. Using these specifications, the ray-tracing program follows each ray backward from the viewer to a pixel on the computer screen and on through each interaction with surfaces in the scene until it reaches the light source. A light ray traversing a scene having many objects and complex reflections could meet more than 1,000 surfaces before it reaches its destination. Consequently, the program must make thousands of calculations in order to display a believable image on the screen. Although ray tracing is a time-consuming and expensive form of computer graphics, it can make objects so realistic that the results are often hard to distinguish from photographs.

The spheres at left are shown in the inset as they might look in a computer image created by a ray-tracing program. Both spheres are made of rays reflected from each alone, but the blue sphere also shows a reflection created by rays that have first bounced off the red one. Tracing rays back from the viewer saves computer time by excluding light rays, such as the ones represented here by dashed lines, that are reflected away from the screen.

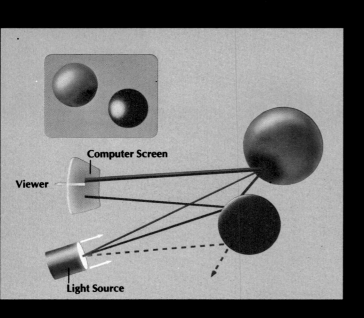

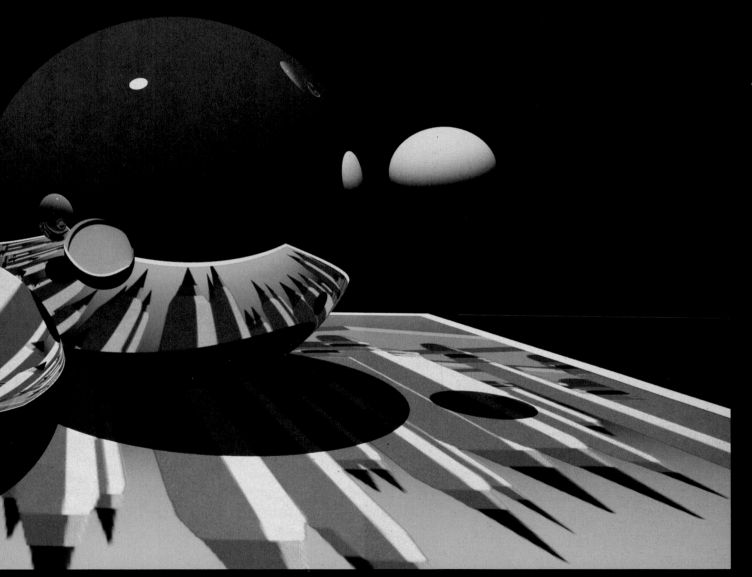

Five hours of calculations were necessary to trace the thousands of light rays that compose the reflections, refractions and shadows in this fanciful computer graphic of spheres floating above a forest of pencils. The sphere that overlaps the purple one is transparent, like glass. Instead of reflecting the pencils, as the others do, it acts as a lens that inverts the scene below it, showing the pencils upright on their eraser ends.

Reproducing Patterns and Textures

Drawing the bumpy skin of an orange or the bricks in a wall receding into the distance is tedious business for pencil-and-paper artists: Not only must each feature be drawn individually but the effects of perspective must be taken into account. Bumps on the orange all differ slightly in shape and must become smaller and closer together near the fruit's edges to make the orange appear spherical. Similarly, bricks in foreground sections of a wall must be larger than bricks in the background. Computer artists are more fortunate. For them, graphics programmers have devised shortcuts that create patterns or textures on three-dimensional objects.

One method, called image mapping, wraps a flat image around an object. For instance, to endow a computer-generated table with a wood-grain pattern, an artist might photograph a flat piece of wood and enter the texture in the computer with a digitizing camera. The mapping program matches the digitized coordinates of the wood pattern to the coordinates of the table, modifying details of the pattern as necessary to retain the table's three-dimensional appearance.

Bump mapping, which creates the illusion of lumpy or wrinkled surfaces, goes a step further. Instead of applying a flat pattern such as wood grain to the object being textured, it uses one with peaks and valleys. Then a lighting program, which simulates a light source and calculates the resulting highlights and shadows, electronically re-creates the texture on the object.

A third kind of mapping, illustrated on these pages, is called spatial texturing. In this technique, a program generates a pattern in three dimensions, which is subsequently mapped throughout the object being textured.

Make-believe Marble in Three Dimensions

The vase on the opposite page, seemingly carved from solid marble, was actually created in four stages with a computer equipped for spatial texturing. Using a solid-modeling program, the artist first constructed a vase, assigning no texture to any of the points within it. Next, a spatial-texturing program helped to fashion a block of "marble" from a simple mathematical expression that the artist altered randomly for an irregular pattern. In the third stage of the operation, the artist instructed the computer to place the vase inside the marble block. Then, after positioning the vase to obtain a satisfactory pattern on its surface, the artist instructed the computer to replace the texture-less features of the original vase with marble.

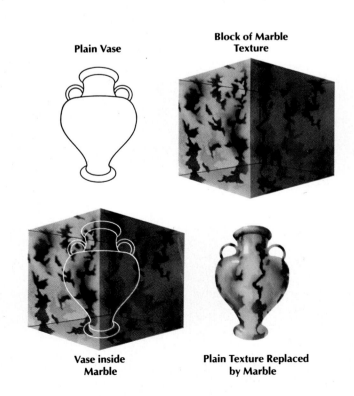

Plain Vase

Block of Marble Texture

Vase inside Marble

Plain Texture Replaced by Marble

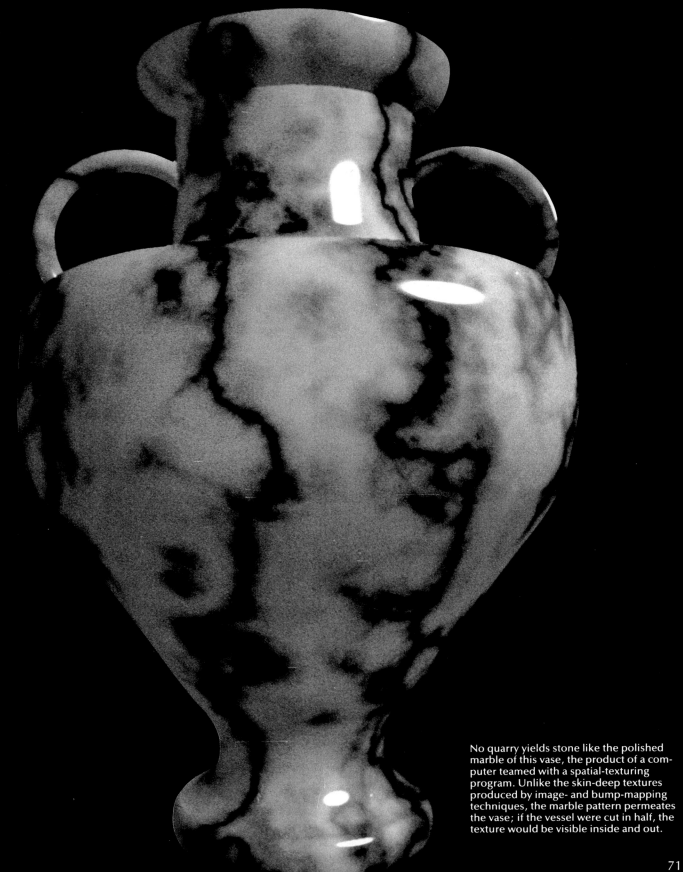

No quarry yields stone like the polished marble of this vase, the product of a computer teamed with a spatial-texturing program. Unlike the skin-deep textures produced by image- and bump-mapping techniques, the marble pattern permeates the vase; if the vessel were cut in half, the texture would be visible inside and out.

Systems for Painting Electronically

Simple and easy to use, paint systems are the graphics tools that come the closest to brush, oil and canvas. With an electronic stylus, a mouse or a puck *(pages 18-21),* an artist selects from a screen-displayed menu of choices a command that turns the control device into a "brush." Another command assigns a color, much as dipping a real brush into paint readies it for use. Then, as the artist moves the device across a table or a digitizing tablet, a swath of color appears on the screen.

Paint systems range from the elementary to the extraordinary. Basic ones are usually limited to 16 or fewer colors, although in some cases these can be combined to form new hues. Moreover, fine detail and smooth, unjagged edges elude such systems, which have coarse-grained monitors that display a total of only 30,000 or so pixels. Because professional artists need more colors and higher resolution, commercial paint systems usually can display more than 4,000 colors on a monitor with a million pixels or more. Painters are then able to create freehand portraits like the one at right. In addition, commercial artists can use a camera or other digitizing device to scan photographs or videotapes into the computer, employing the paint system's color repertoire to combine film seamlessly with artwork.

At its most sophisticated, a painting system joins other rendering and modeling programs in the enormous memory of a mainframe computer. On this scale, paint systems can give artists a versatility and speed unattainable with paints and inks. By combining these tools, an artist can perform such feats as wrapping a painting around a sphere or adding an airbrushed background to an animated sequence.

Artist Mark Lindquist created this portrait with a computer graphics paint system in much the same way that oils are applied to canvas. The image began as a rough, charcoal-like sketch to which the artist then added color, sparingly at first *(top)* but with increasing complexity as the work progressed *(middle and bottom).* "I feel the most fluent, the freest, workng on the computer," said Lindquist. "I love the idea of working with light rather than paints."

Science and the Silver Screen

Inside the animation building on the corner of Mickey Avenue and Dopey Drive, Richard Taylor could see that he had a problem. Once a light-show artist for rock bands, Taylor had made a name for himself designing animation for television commercials. Now he was at Disney Studios in Burbank, California, co-supervising the industry's most exciting special effects project of 1981: the computer movie *TRON*.

As Taylor and his graphics team sat in the animation building's darkened screening room viewing unedited scenes from the preceding day's work, a projector cast the otherworldly image of an actor kneeling beside a crystal pool. Clothed in a luminous, glowing uniform accented by streaks of bright colors, the figure lay down to drink from the pool—and his stomach disappeared. The room dissolved into laughter, Richard Taylor groaned, and the scene was played over and over while he tried to determine what had gone wrong. Finally, he ordered the sequence to be redone, and the screening continued. Minutes later, more giggles rippled through the audience as the screen displayed several actors descending a staircase, alternately walking on thin air or sinking thigh deep into the steps.

In both cases, a common technique from conventional movies—that of super-imposing live action over an artificial background—had misfired. The live characters had been photographed descending real stairs or lying down on real ground; stairs and ground were then replaced by imaginary substitutes created in a computer. But when the real and imaginary images were combined, the fit was slightly askew.

Although the computer-generated images for *TRON* were ambitious, Taylor and his colleagues were by no means the first to adapt computers to the making of movies. The earliest such use of computers was to control

This vivid photograph of billiard balls in motion is in fact no such thing: The balls and their green felt background were produced on a computer screen with specialized graphics software. The techniques required for such realism have been developed largely in response to the demands of film makers, who seek a seamless integration of special effects and live-action photography.

75

the movements of movie cameras. One of the pioneers in this field was inventor John Whitney Sr., whose working studio was the garage at his home in Pacific Palisades, a community approximately 20 miles west of Hollywood. During the 1950s, Whitney had experimented with World War II gun-director mechanisms and analog computers to devise what he called a "technology of the surplus junkyard."

One of Whitney's techniques was to create the illusion of motion by photographing a static painting with a camera that he moved in small increments for each frame. Later the technique was applied to models. An aircraft approaching head on, for example, would appear to bank and fly in the opposite direction if the camera was backed away as the model was simultaneously rotated on its horizontal axis. Controlling the camera with a computer made it possible to repeat such movements precisely, so that a background or a second model photographed on a different strip of film could later be made into a composite without encroaching on the image of the original model. As the practice evolved, techniques like these came to provide most of the special effects for television and science fiction movies.

But the idea of creating a special effect by building and manipulating a model wholly within the computer—computer-generated imagery, or CGI to its practitioners—did not emerge until the early 1970s, when graphics software acquired the versatility necessary to be of use in film and television production. Shortly after that time, in the mid-1970s, *Westworld* and *Futureworld,* two movies about androids escaping from the control of their masters, flirted with computer images to simulate the world as it would be seen through the eyes of a robot.

For *Star Wars,* released in 1977, director George Lucas had one of his special effects men devote three months to creating a 90-second sequence for a briefing scene before the final battle; the audience sees what appears to be a computerized diagram of the interior levels of the Death Star, the evil Empire's planet headquarters. This was in fact the only authentic sample of computer graphics in the film; the computerized cockpit displays that helped pilots fire on enemy

In this frame from the motion picture *TRON,* a trio of futuristic vehicles called Lightcycles traverse a landscape of grids. Each Lightcycle is composed of 57 geometric forms that have been combined by a solid-modeling program. Because they contain fewer basic elements, the cycles were easier to animate than are models created with polygons.

spacecraft were actually produced with conventional animation drawings. Two years later, Disney Studios' science fiction adventure movie *The Black Hole* included 75 seconds of computer-generated imagery: a vortex-shaped grid that threatened to suck the heroes' spaceship into its depths.

These modest beginnings were but a child's dabblings compared with the computer graphics envisaged for *TRON*. Sadly for its creators, the movie would not fulfill its box-office expectations, nor would it receive the critical acclaim that had been hoped for. Yet *TRON* would set a standard for the use of computer graphics in movies that later films, as well as special effects for television, would measure themselves against. What is more, even as *TRON* was being assembled, programmers were at work writing sophisticated graphics software that would break new ground in creating both imaginary scenes and realistic images indistinguishable from photographs. And hardware developments would keep pace as well: In a few years, powerful supercomputers would be able to keep track of the millions of bits of digital information that go into generating a computer image, and film printers would be able to match staircases to actors automatically.

A DETERMINED DUO

The two men behind *TRON* were Steven Lisberger, a 31-year-old animator, and Donald Kushner, a lawyer turned theater producer and movie distributor. In 1978, the two had packed up Lisberger's Boston animation shop and moved it to Southern California to complete *Animalympics,* a cartoon takeoff on the Olympic Games to be held in Moscow in 1980. When the United States decided to boycott the Games, a deal between Kushner and the National Broadcasting Company to air the film fell apart.

In the meantime, Lisberger discovered video games and got an idea for a new movie—a fantasy starring live actors as characters in an electronic world and featuring animation done with computers. Lisberger's idea would evolve into *TRON,* a story about a brilliant but erratic programmer who gets sucked into a computer. There he battles to survive in a hostile world populated with deadly tanks, police robots and human-like characters strikingly reminiscent of people he knew on the outside.

Convinced that financing for *TRON* would have to come from a major film studio, Kushner and Lisberger prepared a detailed presentation, complete with descriptions of characters, a script and plans for making the movie. The project demanded immense faith. "When we were putting the project together," said Kushner later, "the technology to do the computer art we needed didn't actually exist yet. But we were counting on the fact that computer technology was improving so quickly that by the time we were ready to make the movie, it would exist."

When the presentation document was finished, it filled 300 pages stuffed into a loose-leaf binder, which the partners lugged around Los Angeles in a quest for backing. Disney Studios was far down their list of possible financiers. Because of the Disney tradition of hand-drawn animation, the two film makers considered the studio one of the least likely to adopt the concept. But the company had recently named 29-year-old Tom Wilhite as production chief, and the proposal intrigued him. "It was the most interesting idea I'd seen, an entirely new

Simplifying the Art of Animation

Cartoons, the fleeting delight of youngsters on a Saturday morning, can be tedious labor for the adults who create them. Each brief minute that Mickey Mouse scampers across the movie screen requires 1,440 meticulous drawings to give the illusion of fluid motion. Each drawing must be hand-painted on a clear plastic sheet called a cel so that it can later be sandwiched together with background scenery. A 15-minute cartoon might contain 30,000 drawings and take a team of 20 skilled animators, artists, editors and checkers a month or more to produce.

Computers can simplify the animation process and speed it up dramatically. Acting on instructions from a human operator, they can draw and help color as much as 80 percent of the illustrations that go into a cartoon. For example, an artist assisted by a computer can color as many as 500 cels a day instead of the 35 to 40 that could be done by hand. A 15-minute animated movie can be completed in less than a week.

Computer-assisted animation saves an artist time in a number of ways. Once a drawing is entered into the computer, it can be enlarged, reduced or repeated at will. In a process called in-betweening, the computer allows an animator to draw only the key frames of a movement such as that of a bounding deer (right). In doing so, the artist supplies sufficient information for the computer to complete the action by drawing pictures to fit between the key frames.

Coloring the drawings is also more efficient with a computer. By touching a stylus to the screen, an artist can instantly fill an area with a color. If that color proves unsatisfactory, the artist need only press a few keys to replace it with another. To accomplish the same result in coventional animation, the artist must scrape off the old color and repaint with the new.

These eight drawings are part of a 45-frame series that shows a bounding deer. An animator drew the top and bottom pictures—called key frames—by hand, then entered them into a computer, which created the six intervening frames by a process called linear interpolation. In essence, the computer calculated how far the deer's head, body, legs and hoofs would move in each of six equal steps between key frames, then redrew the deer at each stage of the action.

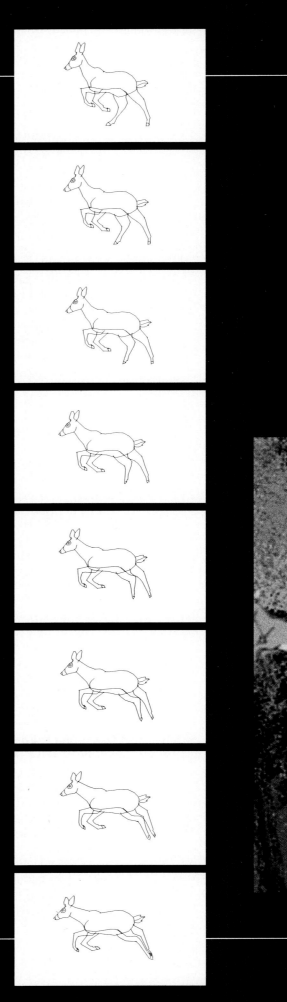

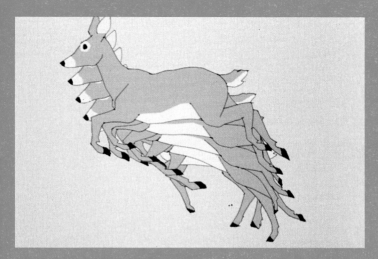

An animator has superimposed on one another five key frames of a deer at various points in midair to confirm that the action will not appear disjointed and has tinted them identically. The artist colors only the key frames; the computer tints the in-between images to match.

What appears to be a herd of deer is actually the gait of a single deer duplicated several times. To keep the herd from seeming to move in unison, the artist can instruct the computer to set the deer and its running cycle at different sizes and locations on the screen, and to stagger the deer's appearances.

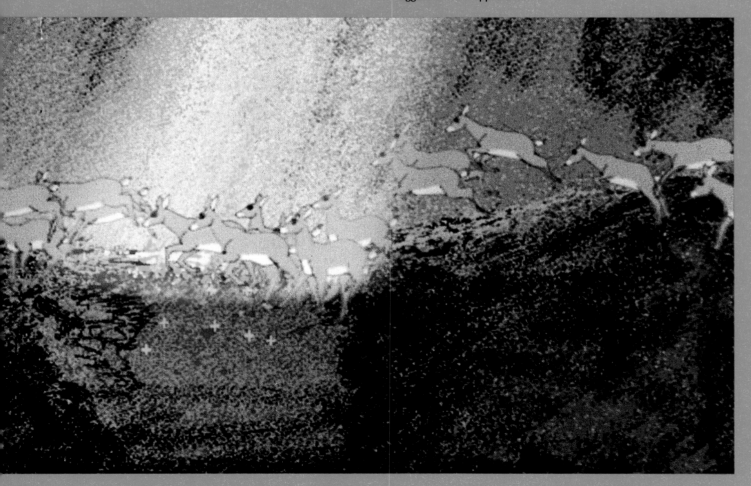

Aided by the computer, the artist combines vibrant colors and a soft, airbrush effect to create a magical setting for the herd of animated deer.

mythology of characters," Wilhite remembered. Moreover, he continued, "we wanted to get back into the risk-taking business at Disney, and *TRON* looked like the perfect project to do it with."

Wilhite's superiors, concerned that the project was overambitious, were considerably less enthusiastic. Yet they, too, were swayed after seeing a two-minute demonstration film that Lisberger had assembled. It proved that Lisberger, an animator by trade, was capable of directing live action, and it showed the feasibility of mixing actors with computer-generated graphics. In April 1981, Kushner and Lisberger got a green light from Disney to begin work.

The computer graphics for the demonstration film had been created by three groups: an Elmsford, New York, company called Mathematical Applications Group, Inc., or MAGI; Information International, Inc., or Triple I, of Culver City, California; and a group from the New York Institute of Technology. And it was from Triple I that Richard Taylor was recruited to help supervise special effects for the movie. Originally, Triple I was to have done all of the computer graphics work for *TRON*. But the company had too little computing power to handle the job and balked at buying more. So MAGI was hired to share the load, and two other firms—Digital Effects, Inc., of New York and Robert Abel & Associates, a Los Angeles firm noted for its award-winning graphics on television—would provide titles and a few scenes.

DYNAMISTS AND IMAGISTS
Had Triple I done all the graphics work for *TRON,* the movie would have turned out much differently than it did. For MAGI and Triple I employed radically dissimilar approaches to computer-generated imagery, approaches that spawned two schools of thought. Dynamists, represented by MAGI, value movement above detail, because that is where MAGI's systems excel. Imagists, represented by Triple I, emphasize the texture and smoothness of the image rather than its motion.

MAGI had developed an imaging system called SynthaVision that contained a library of 25 preformed solid shapes such as cylinders, spheres, pyramids, cones and doughnuts. SynthaVision's software allowed an artist to link these so-called geometrical primitives *(pages 62-63)* into elaborate constructions and then to sculpt them electronically into whatever design was required. Larry Elin, head of MAGI's production team, likened the system to having "a box full of little wooden shapes that you can plunk together to make more complex shapes, with the added attraction that you can also subtract a shape or part of a shape."

SynthaVision's building-block approach to generating computer images resulted in smooth, mechanical-looking objects; except for shading, there was little detail to indicate curving surfaces. However, another feature compensated for this lack of realism. SynthaVision required a relatively small data base to describe even a quite complex object. Thus, images could be computed rapidly, and once computed, they could be displayed on the screen at film speed—that is, fast enough to preview and fine-tune the animation as it would eventually appear on film. Using a "director's language" built into the SynthaVision system, an animator could describe the path that an object was to follow, evaluate the results on the computer display, then correct the path

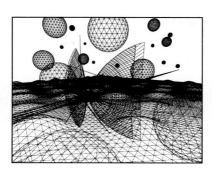

Unlike *TRON's* Lightcycles *(page 76)*, which were made out of simple solid shapes called primitives, the movie's Solar Sailer and its environment were modeled with a mesh of polygons. Designers first sketched the sailer on graph paper, dividing it into triangles, then traced the image on a digitizing tablet to enter it into the computer *(above)*. Rendering programs added color and shading to the finished picture *(right)*. This technique allows for greater detail than does solid modeling but requires vastly more computer memory.

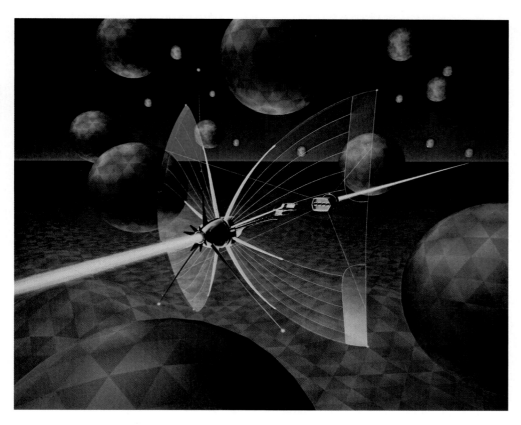

if necessary. This ability to choreograph the movements of objects on the screen suited MAGI's system to the parts of *TRON* that depended on the perfect execution of complex motion. Light cycles—speedy, motorcycle-like vehicles bent on mutual annihilation—could be made to race neck and neck inside one of the movie's ''video game arenas.'' Ominous so-called Recognizer police robots, angular flying arches whose role it was to maintain order, could be made to swoop in formation across *TRON's* computer landscape like mechanical birds of prey.

Triple I's approach to generating images by computer, however, made such choreography difficult. Instead of employing a small number of geometrical primitives to build complex shapes, Triple I artists constructed their images from elaborate linkages of polygons, joined together like tiles in a fine three-dimensional mosaic. Once entered into the computer, the mosaic could be smoothed, shaped, colored, textured and lighted in almost any way that an artist might wish.

The strength of this technique lay in its ability to model details such as distinctive facial features or the parts of imaginary spacecraft *(page 81)* in a convincing manner. But unlike MAGI's primitive solids, each polygon was unique and had to be entered into the computer by the coordinates that defined each of its corners. Moreover, to give the computer a three-dimensional appreciation of the image, three separate sets of coordinates, representing front, side and top views of the

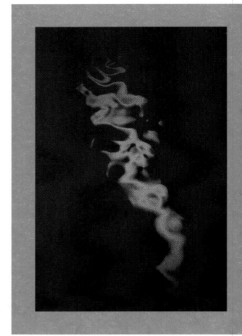

Procedures for Creating Ethereal Effects

Soft-edged, changeable things such as smoke or water are common in nature but difficult to model on the computer with traditional techniques. But programmers are devising ways to generate such images with simple procedures repeated over and over, often with some random variation built in. The smoke at far left was produced by a program that created sine wave shapes and then broke them up, distorted them and dictated a few points where the background would show through. The urn at top left and its background were given their watery texture through a program that assigned a regular pattern of reflections and shadows to the otherwise smooth models. And the bubble at bottom left was created by a program that modeled the transparent colorful effect produced when light diffracts through a soapy surface.

object, had to be recorded. All told, a single object in a frame of film might require the creation of 15,000 polygons—a herculean task that could take a Triple I artist weeks to complete.

Tracking thousands upon thousands of polygons all but overwhelmed Triple I's computer; the more elaborate pictures, requiring shading or other details, could take more than a minute to appear on the screen. This plodding pace made it impractical to preview motion for the movie *TRON* with the Triple I system.

THE HIGH PRICE OF ONSCREEN DAZZLE

In July 1982, *TRON* was finally released. Of the film's 105 minutes, about 15 had been generated entirely by computer, and another 15 combined computer graphics with live action. Actors and actresses wearing black and white costumes were photographed against neutral backgrounds, leaving most of each frame blank. Color and computer images were added to these areas later, a tedious and difficult process that could require, for each frame of the film, dozens of handmade masks to block color from some areas and let it through to others. In an attempt to save money, Disney eventually had the work done in Taiwan, but even at that, the movie went overbudget, costing approximately $20 million to produce.

This expense played a major role in giving *TRON* a black mark in Hollywood. A project that goes overbudget can bring a smile to a producer's lips if it turns out to be a smash hit at the box office. But *TRON,* though dazzling on the screen, was cursed with a weak plot and dull characters. "The story and art for *TRON* developed together," Lisberger said later. "In my mind that was always a crucial thing about the movie. Since we were cooking up this fantasy world from scratch, we relied on the visuals to tell us the story. If somebody did some sketches for a character or an environment that worked from a design standpoint, they went into the script." This dominance of technology over story line, or form over substance, may have been *TRON's* fatal flaw as a motion picture.

When it became clear that the movie had bombed at the box office, Hollywood adopted a wait-and-see attitude toward computer graphics techniques, a disappointing setback for the small but passionate community of computer graphics experts who had counted on the film to throw open studio gates to computer imaging. Instead, the gates almost swung shut. Triple I sold its computer graphics operation, and other graphics outfits went back to television, where advertisers were entranced by CGI and stations were eager to display flashy, computer-generated logos.

HARNESSING A SUPERMACHINE

But *TRON* had "made the crack in the wall," Richard Taylor later remarked. It was, as he put it, "the beginning of a technical renaissance in the film industry."

Two men who found the crack and slipped through were John Whitney Jr., son of the special effects pioneer, and master programmer Gary Demos. Both had worked for Triple I but had quit before production began on *TRON* to found their own company, Digital Productions. As members of the imagist school of CGI, Digital Productions would harness the world's fastest calculating machines—first a Cray = 1/S supercomputer and then its successor, the Cray X-MP—to fashion images that would be as much as 700 times more complex than the most ambitious of *TRON's* computer-generated objects.

Whitney had been discussing such a film since 1981 with his friend Miguel Tejeda-Flores, vice president for film development and acquisition at Lorimar, Inc., the television and movie production studio. But no script then making the rounds in Hollywood had the right mix of story line, space setting and broad audience appeal that the two thought would make a movie suitable for the special effects Whitney had in mind.

Digital Productions had scarcely hung out its shingle when Tejeda-Flores called Whitney to say that a script reader at Lorimar had come across something that seemed made to order. Called *The Last Starfighter,* it told the story of a young video gamesman who is recruited by aliens to save an embattled federation of planets from imminent destruction. Whitney and Demos started negotiations with the studio even before their first computer was installed.

Although the computer images were an important reason for doing the movie, Whitney was determined not to make the same mistake that Lisberger had made with *TRON.* In *The Last Starfighter,* the story came first: "The special effects are there to serve the purpose of furthering that story," Whitney said later. "They were not meant to stand alone as special effects, but to present outer space in as acceptable a way and as easy a way as location photography does."

The centerpiece was a space fighter called the Gunstar. The first step in creating the craft was to make a detailed drawing on graph paper to facilitate encoding it for the VAX 11/782 mainframe used for the initial phases of production. "In the early stages," said Digital Productions' designer Ron Cobb, "we were kind of handicapped in that I had to use geometric primitives to a certain extent." But gradually, Cobb and the crew of computer encoders became more skilled in their work. As the project advanced, Demos—a programming genius if ever one lived—improved the graphics software he had masterminded, and the Gunstar became increasingly detailed. The final version of the craft, which had begun as a sample of Digital Productions' work for Lorimar's approval, comprised 750,000 polygons and took Digital's team of encoders, which at times had as many as 30 members, almost three months to feed into the computer.

"When we have the images encoded," Whitney explained afterward, "the next step is to put them onstage." To begin with, a computer-generated model of the ship was displayed on a vector graphics monitor as a wire-frame outline of polygons that could be moved around the screen with great facility. This allowed Cobb to preview motion on the screen much as MAGI had been able to do with *TRON*. "The technology intervenes or interferes very little," Cobb said. "Instead it's extremely helpful. There's no end of subtlety; you can add to the action because you have full control over the movement of the object."

The ship could be enlarged or reduced in size at will, and—more significant—it could be easily replicated. The original Gunstar may have taken about six months to create from start to finish, but a hangar scene with 14 such ships—10.5 million polygons altogether—required only a few minutes to bring to the screen. But there were problems, nonetheless. Because these images were transparent wire-frame outlines, it was not always possible to tell foreground from background or, in the case of a ship in the distance, even the direction it faced. "We had a few funny instances like that when we had ships passing through things or flying backwards," Cobb recalled.

But all of these details were clarified in the next phase of development, when Digital brought in its heavy hitter: The Cray X-MP. Now Cobb's team could color the surfaces of the wire-frame renditions of the Gunstar at workstations equipped with very-high-resolution raster monitors *(pages 22-23)*. This made it possible, for example, to introduce dents and other blemishes on the spacecraft

A crucial test of realistic computer simulation comes in this scene *(left)* from *The Last Starfighter*, in which the Starcar takes off from earth. Programmers had to craft an image with such high resolution and detail that viewers could not tell the difference when it was combined in the film with footage of an actual car *(below)*.

Bristling with exotic spacecraft, this computer-generated hangar from *The Last Starfighter* vividly demonstrates the advantages of a graphic data base. Using conventional special effects, different ships would have been built at great expense as separate models. With a computer, a designer builds only one image of each kind of ship and then repeats it across the screen as often as necessary.

to keep the ships from looking too much like clones of the original. Digital's software permitted a technical editor to choose from nearly 70 billion colors. Although the human eye cannot distinguish so many shades, without them, changes in surface tones—the subtle gradation from sunlight to shadow, for example—can result in stripes that rob the object of its realism. To further the illusion, the technical editor assigned a given surface type for each group of polygons, creating the sheen of metal or the dullness of wall paint. Finally, much as a stage may be lighted with a spotlight, the Gunstar could be placed in a physical context by telling the computer where to position how many light sources and how bright each should be.

The lights themselves could not be seen, of course, but the effects brought the spacecraft to life. Having established these details for the first frame of film for a scene, the director relied on the computer to apply them to the remaining frames. Each movement of the Gunstar caused its appearance to change as if the fighter were a real object, illuminated by the flash of explosions as it battled through space.

Such realism did not come cheap. To assign a color and a surface to each polygon in an image, and to set the lighting, required the computer to perform between 24 and 72 billion calculations for each frame of the scene. On average, a VAX computer would have needed more than 16 hours to construct each frame of the movie on a workstation monitor—an impossibly unwieldy process for a film that would eventually contain about 36,000 frames of computer-generated imagery. The Cray X-MP accomplished the same task in two and a half minutes.

The Gunstar was so believable the technical director had no qualms about its passing for real on the screen. A far more challenging test of photographic realism

The Complexity of Human Movement

Producing realistic models of the human body in motion is one of the hardest tasks facing computer animators today. A typical human activity—walking, for instance—is a synthesis of hundreds of subtly coordinated movements that include complex rotations of joints, the flexing of muscles from head to toe and reactions to surroundings. The softness and flexibility of the human form are also obstacles for graphics software because of the difficulty of describing such irregularities mathematically.

But many aspects of human motion have been closely studied in such fields as biomechanics and robotics, and data from this research has been used to create animation soft-

(a)

1. RIGHT STANCE LMP/LEFT SWING LMP
2. RIGHT STANCE LMP/LEFT STANCE LMP
3. RIGHT SWING LMP/LEFT STANCE LMP
4. RIGHT STANCE LMP/LEFT STANCE LMP

(b)

1. HIP FLEXION, KNEE FLEXION, ANKLE FLEXION
2. HIP FLEXION, KNEE EXTENSION, ANKLE FLEXION
3. HIP EXTENSION, KNEE EXTENSION, ANKLE EXTENSION

(c)

1. DOWNWARD PELVIC CORONAL ROTATION ABOUT SUPPORT HIP, HIP EXTENSION, KNEE FLEXION, ANKLE EXTENSION, SUPPORT ROTATION ABOUT HEEL
2. UPWARD PELVIC CORONAL ROTATION ABOUT SUPPORT HIP, FORWARD TRANSVERSE ROTATION ABOUT SUPPORT HIP, HIP EXTENSION, KNEE FLEXION, ANKLE FLEXION
3. UPWARD PELVIC CORONAL ROTATION ABOUT SUPPORT HIP, FORWARD PELVIC TRANSVERSE ROTATION ABOUT SUPPORT HIP, HIP EXTENSION, KNEE EXTENSION, ANKLE FLEXION
4. FORWARD PELVIC TRANSVERSE ROTATION ABOUT SUPPORT HIP, HIP EXTENSION, KNEE FLEXION, ANKLE EXTENSION, SUPPORT ROTATION ABOUT BALL OF FOOT
5. HIP FLEXION, KNEE FLEXION, ANKLE EXTENSION

(d)

1. ELBOW FLEXION, SHOULDER FLEXION

(e)

1. ELBOW EXTENSION, SHOULDER EXTENSION

Some of the complex elements of a walking sequence are revealed in this list of motions from the skeleton animation cycle. Section (a) details the local motor programs, or LMPs, that go into the overall walk control program. The leg swing LMP is shown in (b), lower body stance LMP in (c), forward arm swing LMP in (d) and rearward arm swing LMP in (e).

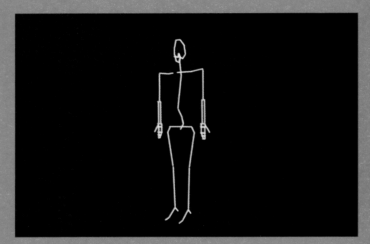

To refine motion control in an animated sequence before rendering a fully shaded raster version, the programmer calls up a stick figure version on a vector monitor and puts it through a series of tests.

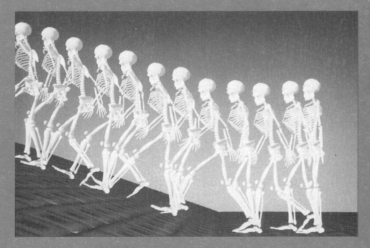

After the sequence passes the stick figure test, it is rendered in color on a raster monitor. This composite image shows 12 frames—one for each skeleton—from a film depicting the skeleton's response to uneven terrain.

ware such as the walking skeleton system shown on these pages. Here, the programmer chose to avoid the difficulties of working with fully fleshed figures by using a model consisting of rigid segments. The problems of coordinating a multitude of motions were dealt with by organizing the programs in three levels. At the top level is the task manager, which, after receiving a description of the task to be performed—say, "crouch, jump and walk forward"—will break the action down into a sequence of skills. The second level controls the programs for each skill—the motions involved in crouching, for example. The third level consists of local motor programs, each of which controls a set of joints for one motion, such as bending knee, hip and ankle during crouching. As the programs are executed, they update the skeleton data base so that each new movement starts from the correct position.

The ability to produce accurate models of bodies in action holds great promise, not only for film makers but for doctors, athletes, dancers and others concerned with the movement of the human form. But even with the most sophisticated equipment, the complexities of programming a realistic human figure to execute even a simple dance step can make the modeling of a starship battle in outer space look easy.

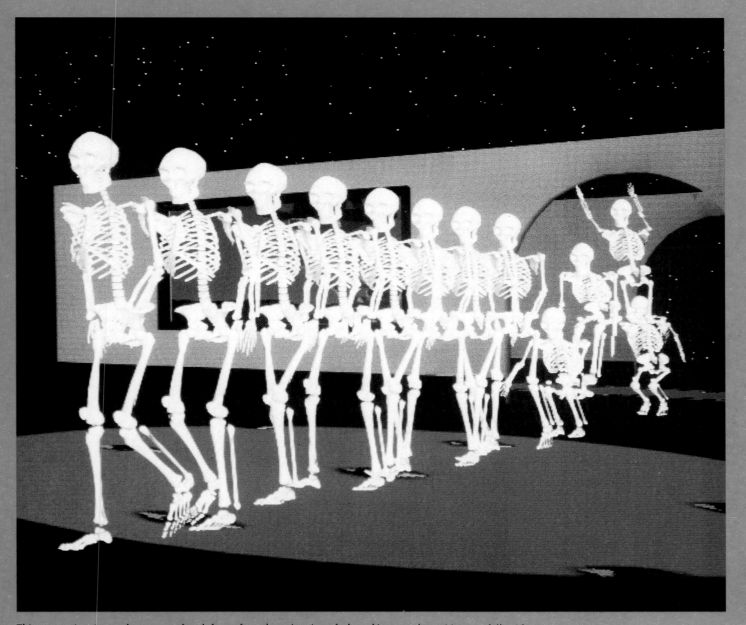

This composite picture shows every fourth frame from the animation of a broad jump and transition to a full stride.

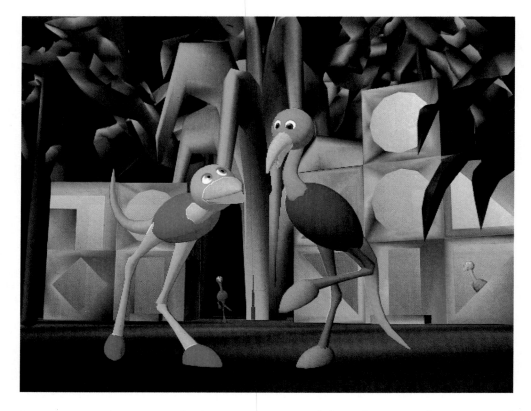

The personalities of the snobbish Snoot *(right)* and the roguish Muttly *(left),* characters in a computer-animated film, are revealed by the way the two birds move. Complex programs govern the articulation and distinctive motions of each figure's eyes, head, neck, body, leg joints and tail.

in a computer image was the Starcar, an automobile in the movie that converted into a spaceship. According to Demos, after the car was designed, it was actually "built" in the computer first. Then the real car, a drivable mock-up, was constructed from the same plans by a Modesto, California, custom builder, using a Volkswagen van chassis stretched 14 inches.

Demos recalled the widespread concern that the physical model and the computer model would compare unfavorably when the film cut from one to the other—and the relief when the project turned out all right: "We took a bunch of photographs of the simulated one and the real one and we showed them to Ron Cobb, who had designed the car, and he couldn't tell which was which. To be quite honest, I couldn't tell which was which, either, and I knew we were in pretty good shape when things like that started to happen."

The last phase of making the movie was to transfer the computer images to film. Each frame was photographed with a high-resolution film recorder *(pages 28-29),* a process that took from two and a half to five minutes per frame. The Cray could perform this task with virtually no human intervention, so the machine was used for various other operations during the day and left to do the filming at night, with only one person standing by. This phase took six to eight months, and at first kept the supercomputer occupied eight hours a night weekdays and 24 hours a day on weekends; toward the end, it was busy around the clock.

The Last Starfighter was not a blockbuster by Hollywood standards—it cost $14 million to make and grossed only $21 million in its first 31 days—but it earned enough to be considered a success. Perhaps most important, the film demonstrated that computer images could hold their own in a movie that made frequent transitions between real and simulated scenes. "At least a third of the effects in the film attain photorealism," said Cobb. "They are almost flawless. The average filmgoer who is not terribly concerned with the techniques behind the film will probably just assume that these dynamic, interesting images are models—which is extraordinary."

FIGHTING HOLLYWOOD'S SKEPTICS
The success of *The Last Starfighter,* while welcome, did not suddenly turn CGI into a movie industry darling. Both the cost of photographic realism and the skepticism of film studios remained high. Television was another matter. For one thing, titles for network specials and the like last only a few seconds, and most commercials are on the screen for no more than 30 seconds. More significant, the low-resolution television screen demands far fewer calculations than the movie screen. Thus, even if the goal is an image as believable as a photograph, such an image can be produced for television in a fraction of the time—and for a small percentage of the cost—required to create the same image for a film.

One who refused to give up on CGI for the movies was George Lucas, head of Lucasfilm, Ltd., and creator of the wildly successful series of *Star Wars* movies. In 1979, Lucas had formed a computer division within Lucasfilm, with a mandate to "bring high technology into the film industry." For starters, he raided the computer graphics laboratory of the prestigious New York Institute of Technology, hiring the four men who had set up the school's computer graphics lab in 1974: Edwin Catmull, Alvy Ray Smith, Malcolm Blanchard and David DiFrancesco. The results were impressive.

This realistic forest scene is a backdrop for the computer-animated film *The Adventures of André & Wally B.,* featuring an android and a bee. Trees, grass and flowers were all generated with particle systems *(page 64)* employing random variables that introduced natural-looking irregularities. A shading program dappled the trees with sunlight and cast tree shadows on the grass.

Among other accomplishments, the group created a computer-animated short subject to showcase at the 1984 International Animation Festival in Toronto. The film, titled *The Adventures of André & Wally B.*, recounted the adventures of an android named André and a bumblebee named Wally B. living deep in a Disney-style forest executed in such detail that the audience could pick out individual leaves on trees. So voluminous were the graphics calculations for the forest and for the two characters' actions that to produce the film required the power of six Cray central processing units, as well as 15 smaller machines. The finished movie lasted only a minute and a half on the screen.

Then, in the spring of 1985, the Lucasfilm computer whizzes unveiled a graphics computer of their own, which promised to reduce drastically the cost of lifelike computer images. Called the Pixar, the machine consists of four processors for the display, one each to control red, green and blue, and the fourth to control text. Each processor is capable of handling 10 million instructions per second. But the key to Pixar's sophistication and power is its software—intricate algorithms for generating the forms and textures of real life.

The Pixar's graphics abilities, and its relatively low cost—around $100,000, compared with the $10- to $15-million Cray X-MP—make it attractive outside the film industry as well. Hospitals see in it the potential to increase radically the quality of the images produced by CT and PET scanners *(page 46)*. Gas- and oil-exploration companies, which would benefit by clearer pictures of information yielded by seismic soundings of the earth's crust, are also interested in the machine.

As good as the Pixar is, it could not represent the state of the art in computer graphics for long. Indeed, no sooner had Lucas' organization completed work on the Pixar than it announced an even more capable machine for 1986, the Reyes. The special-purpose graphics machine has complex algorithms built into its hardware, making it as much as 1,000 times faster than either the Pixar or the Cray X-MP. Thus the acronym the Lucas team fondly attached to Reyes: Renders Everything You Ever Saw. In time, as computer graphics specialists adapt advances in computer hardware to CGI, it is reasonable to expect speed to increase as prices fall. Ultimately the work that once required a Cray might be accomplished just as quickly with a small computer sitting on a desktop.

Easing the Architect's Burden

Just as the designer of special effects for television and film must spend hours building up a scene element by element, architects must pay close attention to the myriad details that go into the creation of any structure, from a three-story office building to a multimillion-dollar skyscraper. Behind the precise drawings and scale models that are the traditional results of an architect's efforts lie hours of painstaking labor. The simplest design requires several kinds of specialized input, from initial architectural sketches to the technical considerations of engineers of various stripes (structural, mechanical, electrical, civil) and the esthetic concerns of interior designers. Drawings are subject to numerous revisions, and more often than not a change in one plan has repercussions throughout a series of related plans.

The advent of computer-aided design has greatly simplified this process. By taking advantage of a computer's memory capacity, its speed and its ability to organize masses of information, an architectural firm can drastically reduce the time it spends on a project. One pioneer in the infant field of computer-aided architecture is the firm of Skidmore, Owings & Merrill, whose computer-generated designs appear on the following pages. The company's system includes several high-speed minicomputers linked to more than 200 individual terminals. Half of these terminals are graphics workstations with their own keyboards, monitors, digitizing tablets and other input devices. Data-management software designed by the company controls hundreds of applications programs, from two-dimensional drafting to energy analysis. Information for current projects is kept in a central computer file, to which all terminals have access. As a result, one worker can lay out an electrical wiring plan while another examines a variety of window treatments.

Architectural firms that cannot afford to have their systems made to order often use integrated hardware and software packages available from computer graphics vendors. Smaller companies that wish to automate the indispensable but tedious chore of simple drafting make use of desktop microcomputers linked to digitizing equipment.

Manipulating a Wire-Frame Model

In a noncomputerized architect's office, creating a model of a proposed structure means sculpting it out of materials such as plastic or steel, painting it, mounting it on a stand and perhaps photographing it from various angles to show the client. Revising or correcting the model can sometimes mean starting over from scratch. With a computer, an architect can first build the model electronically, storing relevant information in the machine's memory. To display the model from any angle or demonstrate the results of engineering tests, the architect has only to issue a few commands and the appropriate image appears on the computer screen. To make design changes, the architect enters new information in the machine; the computer takes care of integrating it and generates a revised model when necessary.

The range of things the computer can do with the model depends on the architect's software and hardware. Simple graphics packages produce two-dimensional images, useful for the flat plans that make up 95 percent of a draftsman's work. More sophisticated programs enable the computer to generate three-dimensional images, projecting not only the height and width of a structure but its depth as well.

Wire-frame drawings, such as those shown here, are the most basic way to depict a structure in three dimensions. Often displayed on vector monitors (pages 22-23), wire-frame drawings reveal all of a building's outlines simultaneously. With other software packages, a designer can define a building by its surfaces rather than by its outlines. The designer may then command the computer to color in the surfaces facing the viewer and eliminate those that would normally be hidden—creating an image that looks solid.

Once the various dimensions of a building are entered in the computer's memory, the machine is able to show the building from virtually any perspective. Architects thus can explore environmental questions such as how the building would look against an existing skyline, where its shadow might fall at 5 p.m. or whether it would block the view of someone in the building behind it.

Computer graphics enable the architects at Skidmore, Owings & Merrill to stroll down Chicago's Michigan Avenue without leaving their seats. Their computers generate a complete three-dimensional model of downtown Chicago by drawing from a massive data base that includes the outer dimensions of every structure. Displayed on a vector monitor, the model can be viewed at any point and from any perspective at the twist of a dial.

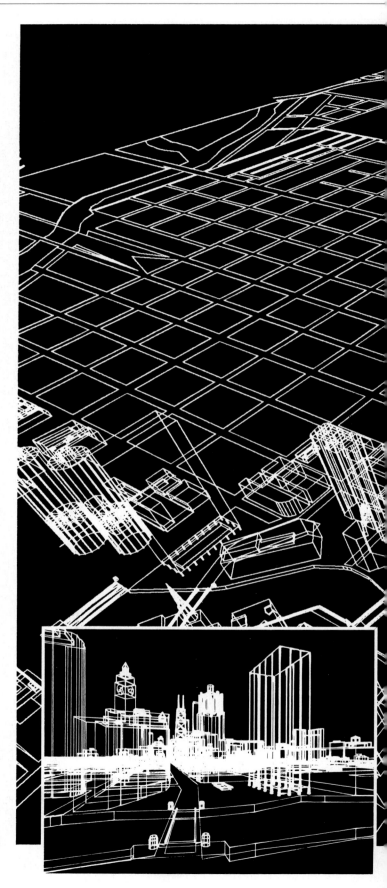

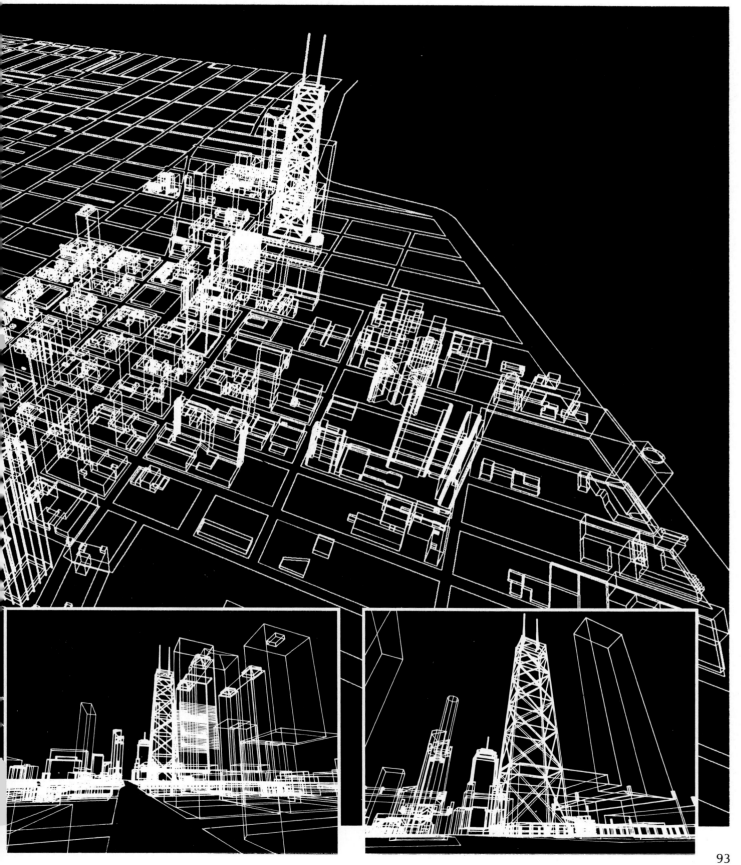

Building a Data Base from the Ground Up

One of the greatest advantages of using a computer in architecture is that the machine can maintain a central graphics file, or data base, and make it available to everyone working on a project. The core element of this file is the floor plan, which serves architects and engineers as the outline for what will eventually become a highly detailed model. The file will ultimately comprise an enormous number of elements, including interior partitions, plumbing and ventilation ducts. At any time, members of the project team can check their designs against others for potential conflicts. Supervisors may also call up one plan and overlay it with several others in order to generate a composite image *(opposite, bottom)* that clarifies the relationships of different parts of the project.

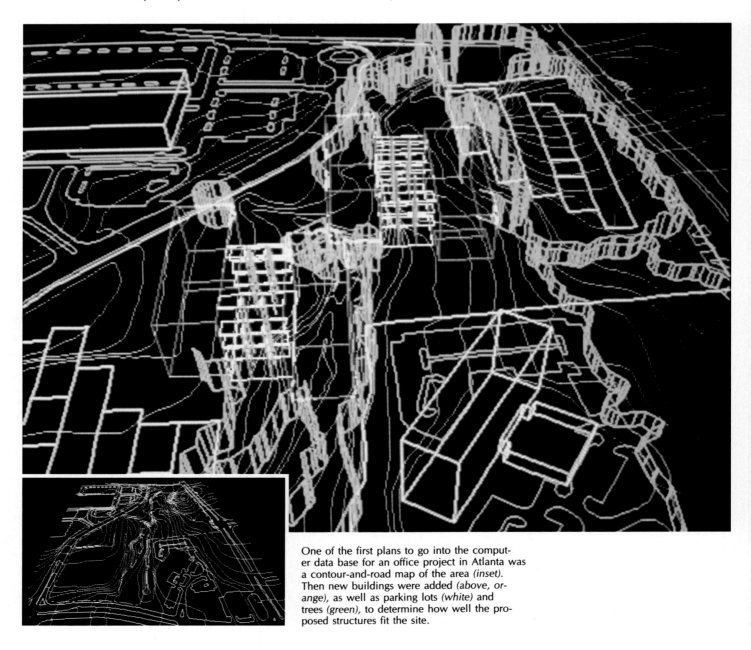

One of the first plans to go into the computer data base for an office project in Atlanta was a contour-and-road map of the area *(inset)*. Then new buildings were added *(above, orange)*, as well as parking lots *(white)* and trees *(green)*, to determine how well the proposed structures fit the site.

In an early floor plan for one of the buildings, the preliminary core (stairs and elevators), the locations of columns, and the perimeter are the only details.

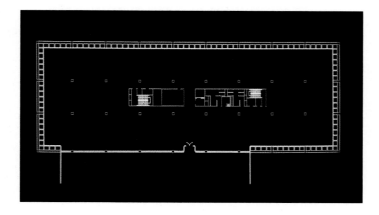

To test the building's warm-weather insulation, the architect specified a time of day and applied a thermal engineering program to plans called up from the central file. The test revealed some heat penetration *(orange)* on the west side.

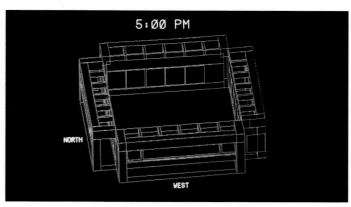

A detail of one of the building's corners shows several plans displayed simultaneously. Lighting fixtures *(orange)*, partitions *(blue)* and ductwork *(green)* were overlaid on the original floor plan *(white)*.

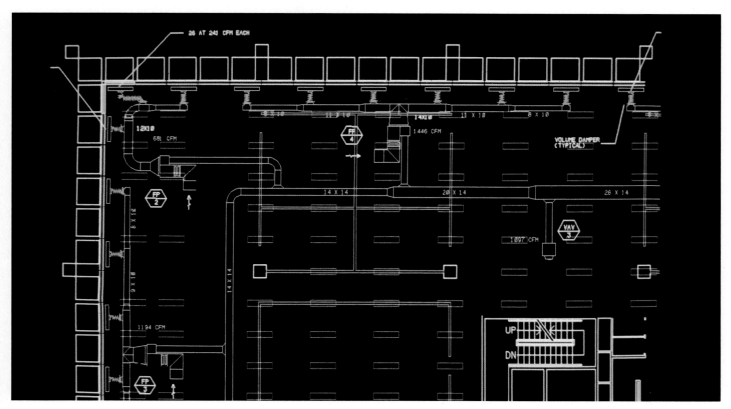

A Powerful Tool for Innovation

Once information on such elements as floor plans, engineering specifications and interior designs has been stored in a project's central data base, architects and engineers are able to create a number of highly elaborate models. For example, engineers can use programs that translate information about building materials and load-bearing capabilities into overlapping images that demonstrate the effect of an earthquake on a building's structural integrity. If a client wants to select from a variety of materials for a building's façade, the computer will generate a model of the structure finished in wood, brick, stone or marble. And if an architect wants to focus on a project's profile, powerful software can build a model of the structure in color while creating wire-frame images of the existing background *(right)*.

Without a computer to generate a stream of images from a master model, an architectural team would spend enormous amounts of time recalculating and redrawing the project. True, data needed to create the original model may take as long to enter into the computer as it would take simply to draw the structure by hand. But finished plans, and any intermediate tests and models, can be generated many times faster, allowing the designer to concentrate on creative thinking and innovative solutions.

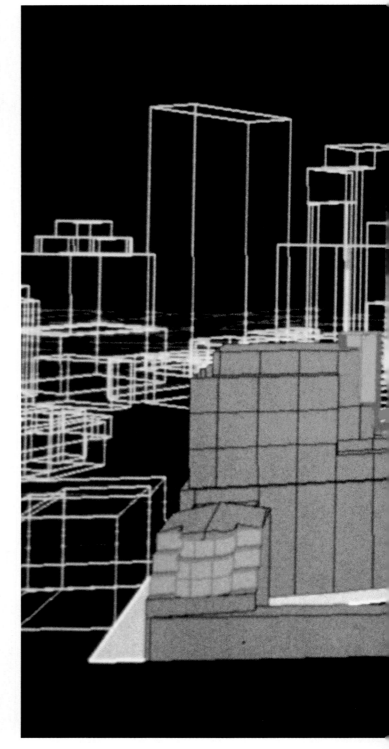

The main challenge presented by Rowes Wharf, a commercial building planned for the waterfront in Boston, was to design a structure that would blend esthetically with the city. Architects thus spent much of their computer time creating models such as this one—a view of the wharf with its surfaces filled in, integrated with a wire-frame view of the Boston skyline.

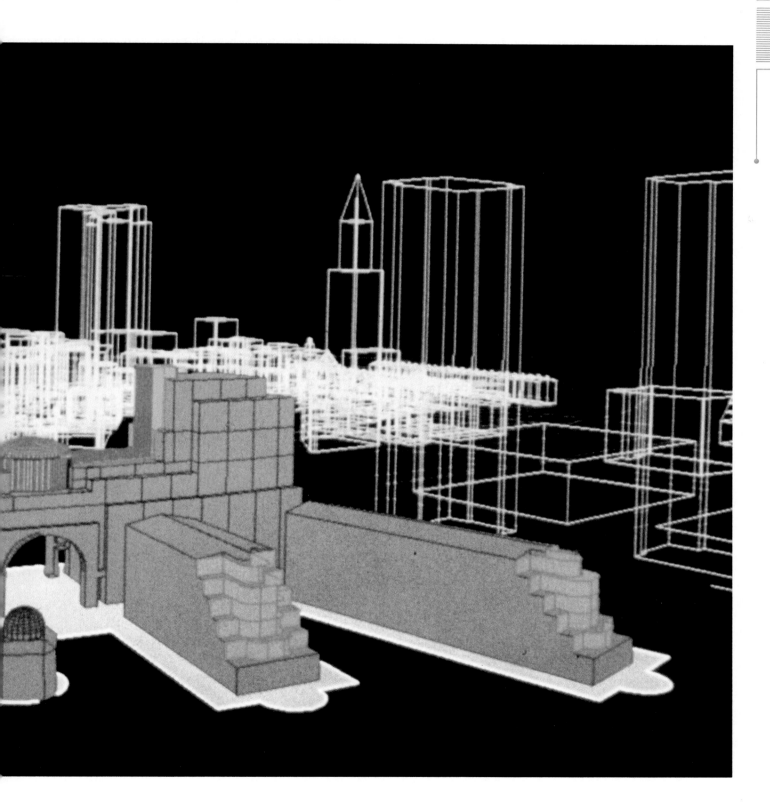

With information from the central data base, the computer can generate a three-dimensional wire-frame image that reveals in exaggerated fashion (red) the effects of wind stress.

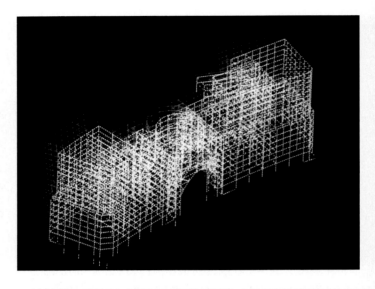

Fundamental engineering data in the computer's master file can create an image like this one, depicting structural elements in a corner of Rowes Wharf, with arrows to indicate the orientations of columns and beams.

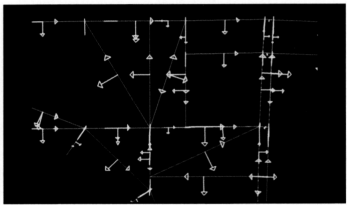

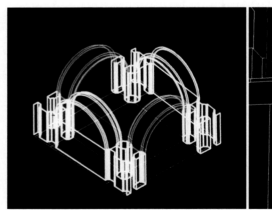

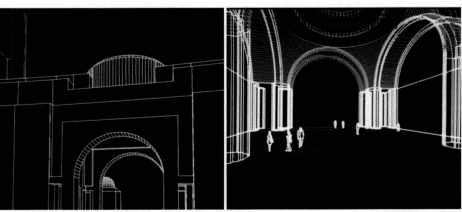

By combining information from the original data base in new ways, an architect can produce studies that allow for esthetic as well as structural evaluation. These views of the dome of Rowes Wharf include a wire-frame study of the arch supports (above), a portrait of the exterior (center) and a wire-frame outline of interior space (right).

To generate this realistic rendering of the finished wharf, an artist called up a model and designated surfaces, colors, angle of light and point of view.

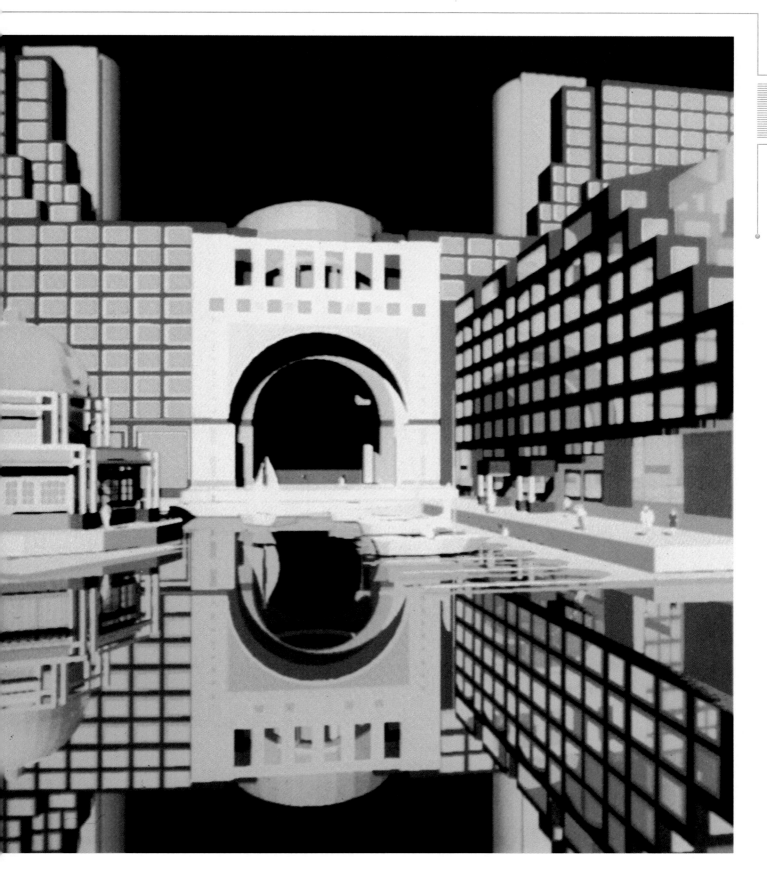

Exploring Artificial Realities

The patient was real enough—a young boy with a severe limp—but the presence of a video camera and a computer terminal made the setting an improbable one for major orthopedic surgery. As the boy limped back and forth in front of the camera, his image appeared on the computer's monitor. At the terminal was Ali Seireg, a University of Wisconsin professor of mechanical engineering, who kept touching the screen with a light pen to make marks on the boy's moving image. A few minutes later, a skeletal figure appeared on the screen. It was a computer-generated model of the child's motions, and it limped just as the boy did.

Then the "surgery" began. Seireg typed in a command to display an enlarged view of one of the figure's legs. Using the light pen as a scalpel, he began to shorten the leg, simulating the removal of small sections of bone. Periodically, Seireg stopped and typed commands to make the figure walk. When it no longer limped, Seireg typed in other commands and the figure ran smoothly across the screen.

Seireg sent the boy's orthopedic surgeon the data on how much bone had been excised from the simulated leg. The information guided the surgeon during the actual operation, augmenting his own expertise and experience. A few months afterward, the boy was able to walk without a noticeable limp for the first time in his life. "I might have achieved the same results without the data," the surgeon said later, "but it was reassuring to first be able to 'try' the operation several times on the computer."

Simulated surgery is one of myriad new applications made possible by modern computer graphics. Unlike computer-generated special effects for movies, television and video games, in which images are the final products, these applications help solve problems in practically every field of endeavor—from science and medicine to business and industry, from the fields of war to the fields of sport.

This look into the sunlit atrium of Raffles City—a planned office, hotel and convention center in Singapore—is just one frame from a computer-generated film that takes the viewer on a tour of the building. Drawing on the fields of architecture, interior decoration and lighting, artist Darcy Gerbarg used blueprints of the actual building to produce her own version of the interior through computer-aided design.

All such applications stem from the unparalleled power of computer graphics to explore what one researcher calls "artificial realities." With appropriate graphics hardware and software, users can create and display electronic models as simple as a two-dimensional business chart or as staggeringly complicated as a three-dimensional molecule of protein, which may consist of thousands of atoms.

Moreover, not only can an individual image be rotated, enlarged and altered, but different models can be made to interact. A computer-generated design of a new automobile shock absorber, for example, can be subjected to the impact caused by a simulated pothole. Or, as in Ali Seireg's simulated surgery, an impaired walk can be compared with the model of a normal gait stored in the computer.

Though many applications still employ the faster and cheaper wire-frame method of drawing, solid-modeling techniques are becoming increasingly widespread (page 62). Unlike the sketchy and sometimes difficult-to-read wire-frame diagrams, solid models depict a wealth of shading and other detail that can render them virtually indistinguishable from reality. This realism—made possible by the television-like method of raster display—is vital to such applications as precision manufacturing and the training of pilots in flight simulators.

AN INDUSTRIAL BOON

The economic impact of computer graphics is greatest in industry, especially in manufacturing. In their most prosaic application, computer images have rendered the drafting table nearly obsolete by producing in only a day precise mechanical drawings that once required a week of tedious manual effort.

But graphics now penetrate all three phases of computerized manufacturing, from conceptualizing the product to actually making it. Computer-aided design (CAD) shortens the design cycle by permitting manufacturers to shape new products on a monitor without first having to build costly physical prototypes. Computer-aided engineering (CAE) subjects the design to extensive analysis and testing that might be too expensive or not even practicable in the real world. And computer-aided manufacturing (CAM) makes use of computer images in automating the machines that fabricate the finished goods.

In any or all of these phases, computer graphics contribute to the manufacture of everything from wide-bodied aircraft and mammoth ship hulls to carpets and running shoes. Many products—among them computer microchips and a brand of potato chips—owe their very existence to computer images. Design and verification of the intricate microscopic circuits that power computers depend upon precise visualization. So, too, do the ridges that give Frito-Lay's O'Grady's potato chips just the right tensile strength to withstand the stress of being plunged into a bowl of cheese dip yet still crunch pleasingly in the consumer's mouth.

Above all, manufacturers prize the enormous gains in productivity made possible by computer simulations. For example, the housing for a common electric can opener is typically made of plastic, which is formed, one housing at a time, in a reusable metal mold. For a manufacturer of can openers, productivity thus depends in no small part on what might seem a trivial consideration: the amount of time required for the molten plastic to cool in

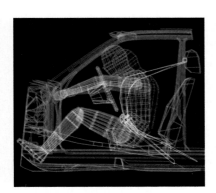

Hurled forward by the impact of a head-on crash at about 30 miles per hour, the human figure in this computer-generated simulation tests the behavior of a seat belt under stress. Such computer-aided engineering techniques are widely used in the automobile industry to develop new design and engineering concepts.

the mold. With the help of CAD, designers at General Electric created a new mold that saved the manufacturer of the can openers $150,000 a year by cooling the molten plastic in less than half the time formerly needed. Computer-aided design also saved GE money by allowing the design job to be completed in hours rather than the weeks normally required for manual drawing and the building of physical models.

AUTOMOTIVE SHORTCUTS

Nowhere are such gains more sought after than in the largest sector of manufacturing, the automobile industry. With huge investments in hardware and software—hundreds of millions of dollars, marks and yen—auto makers are betting on computer graphics to help them stay competitive in the worldwide productivity race. In American, German and Japanese auto centers, designers and engineers labor at thousands of workstations (each costing $100,000 or more) to style and test next year's models and to prepare the tools that will manufacture them.

The creation of a new car still typically begins in the time-honored way. Stylists fashion a full-size replica of the proposed auto from great globs of clay. Until recently, this first step would set in motion a laborious sequence aimed at transforming the clay replica into a plaster cast; traditionally, dies formed from the cast were used to stamp metal sections for the finished auto. At Ford, designers would copy the configuration of the clay model by applying cardboard templates only five inches square to every patch of it. They would then make drawings from the cardboard, transfer these to aluminum templates and arrive at the wooden replica that was the basis for the plaster cast. For every new model of car, thousands of templates jammed the storerooms.

Now, at Ford and elsewhere, the use of computer graphics eliminates the template process. Instead, an electronic device scans the clay model and translates every curving surface into digital values. This mathematical representation is then fed into a computer, where special programs convert it into images that portray the proposed model from every angle. Meanwhile, designers and engineers use a similar process, incorporating data from other sources, to create electronic models of most of the car's components, from camshaft to shock absorbers. Though wire-frame diagrams are adequate for drawing the vehicle's overall configuration, solid-model techniques are essential for designing many of the components, providing a more accurate picture of the parts—inside and out. A solid model also permits calculation of such characteristics as weight, volume and center of gravity.

With the preliminary designs complete, the tinkering begins and CAD comes into its own. Designers can change a shape, almost instantaneously, without having to build a new clay replica to visualize the results. To add a molding to a fender, a designer calls up a menu of options on the screen, uses a light pen to select "wheel opening" and instructs the computer to zoom in on this section of the car. The designer then uses the light pen to draw a cross section of the proposed molding and commands the computer to fit the molding to the fender.

Meanwhile, engineers begin the second stage, computer-aided engineering, to subject designs to all manner of computer simulations. These test whether a given plan works as intended and can help in the evaluation of alternative versions. Some simulations involve tests of vehicle configuration—to discover, for example, how a particular shape will react to the wind at 50 miles per hour. Programs based on data from traditional wind-tunnel tests can simulate lines of air pressure flowing over the car, showing the areas of maximum resistance.

The configuration of interior space is also evaluated. Engineers at General Motors, for example, used to have to build a wooden mock-up of a car's trunk and load it with real suitcases. Now, an engineer loads a computer simulation of the trunk by selecting from menu options such as "golf bag" and "lady's overnight." If everything does not fit, the trunk goes back for redesign. Similar tests are made to evaluate the comfort and safety of drivers and passengers. At Chrysler, so-called human-factors engineers have the help of an electronic human stand-in nicknamed Cyberman. Formerly drawn in wire-frame but now a more realistic solid model, Cyberman sits in a computer mock-up of the driver's seat and moves its flexible joints to test features of interior layout such as legroom and positioning of armrests. Cyberman can be scaled to various human proportions, including those of a female, in which case it is known as Cyberwoman. The model can even be duplicated to serve as passengers, each of which can be individually manipulated.

PLOTTING AREAS OF STRESS

Other tests subject individual components of the auto to computer versions of real-world stress to verify the design or determine what modifications are needed. "We fix parts before the car is built," says Thomas Roberts of the advance design department at GM's Buick, Oldsmobile and Cadillac Divisions. A key method for such testing, known as finite element method (FEM), can evaluate every area of an auto part's structure for strength, vibration and other characteristics. For example, to perform a FEM on the bracket that attaches a stabilizer bar to the frame of a vehicle, an engineer calls up an image of the bracket on the screen. The bracket, which is essential to the smooth handling of an automobile, appears on the screen as a spidery web of lines and curves. Points of intersection called nodes represent areas that will be subjected to simulations of loads the bracket would experience in actual operation. A color stress plot can pinpoint areas most in need of strengthening as well as unstressed areas where reinforcement might be reduced without sacrificing structural integrity. By shaving metal from parts that are stronger than necessary, engineers not only reduce overall weight, which in turn improves the vehicle's fuel mileage, but help cut production costs. Ford, for example, stripped 400 pounds from one of its 1986 models by using FEM to evaluate plastics, graphite and other lightweight materials.

FEM and other methods also enable engineers to test the performance of entire systems. In an evaluation of a vehicle's suspension system at General Motors, for instance, a wire-mesh model looking like an animated blueprint jolts along a make-believe road strewn with potholes and bumps. The vehicle's vibrations are purposely exaggerated on the screen to zero in on specific areas of concern.

Engineers can even visualize how a vehicle holds up in a simulated accident. Staging a real accident obviously costs money. At Ford, a typical test of crash-worthiness used to involve backing a hand-built prototype into a concrete-and-metal barrier at 31 miles per hour. These prototypes cost $300,000 each—an investment that was demolished in less than $1/10$ of a second. Ford engineers can now stage the same crash on a video screen in color graphics. Using

FEM and data based on actual crash tests, they compute the behavior of successive sections of the car's rear end as they crumple during the simulation. "Color graphics enable the engineer to 'peel away' the exterior sheet metal and view the car from any angle to observe what is happening to the inner structure," says a Ford spokesman. "This is something we cannot do with a prototype."

Even after the completion of design and engineering—CAD and CAE—the role of computer graphics continues. Several aspects of the final stage, manufacturing, owe a debt to the design images that are stored in the computer in digital form. This information provides a valuable data base upon which to design—again, with the help of CAD—the tools, dies or molds that will actually manufacture the part. In addition, design data for a given component can control the machine tools that make the part: The data is transferred to paper or magnetic tape, which programs the automated machine. Auto makers also use systems that employ robots, equipped with microcomputers for brains, to weld, drill and perform other tasks with information taken from the original component design process.

Besides contributing to a gain in productivity, computer graphics in the manufacturing stage can help engineers save on raw material. At Ford, engineers have used the computer model of a body-panel component to determine the most cost-efficient way to stamp the port from a large sheet of metal. The result: a saving of $187,000 in metal that ordinarily would have wound up on the scrap

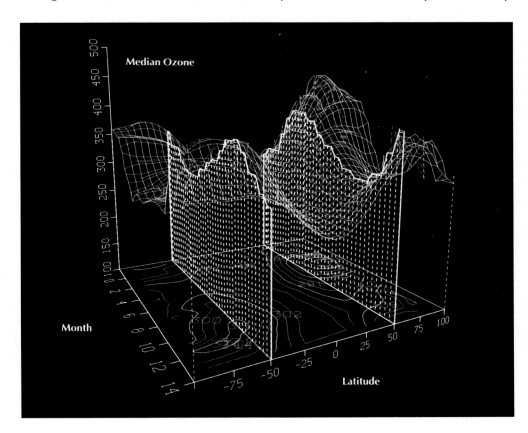

The complex relationship between the amount of ozone in the atmosphere, the latitude and the time of year is neatly summarized in this three-dimensional graph. The advantages of presenting such information in a quickly grasped visual form have made graphs and charts one of the fastest-growing segments of the computer graphics industry.

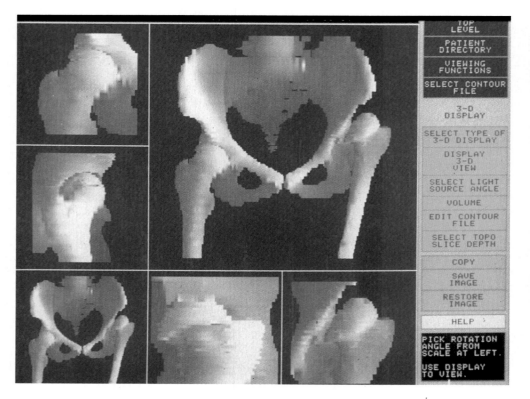

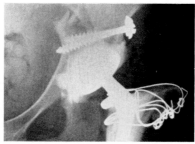

Design for a New Body
Multiple windows from a medical graphics program help a surgeon plan an operation on the displaced left hip of a young woman. After calling up a three-dimensional image of the pelvic area, constructed from two-dimensional CT scans, the surgeon examines both the healthy hip joint *(top left window)* and the displaced hip *(near left, bottom row)* before designing a prosthetic hip joint *(above, top)*. Augmented with necessary bone grafts during surgery, the prosthesis fits perfectly *(above)*.

heap. The goal of auto makers and other industrial leaders is to combine design, engineering and manufacturing into one continuous computerized system. They call such integration CIM, for computer-integrated manufacturing, and envision factories in which everything from design and scheduling to production and shipping is computerized on the same enormous data base. CIM, predicts a report by an agency of the U.S. government, "has more potential to radically increase productivity than any development since electricity."

For now, CIM is relatively rare except in the aerospace industry. There, sections of labyrinthine hydraulic tubing for aircraft are fabricated automatically at the push of a button on the same computer terminal where they were designed.

The aerospace industry has been a pacesetter in the growth of computer graphics in other ways as well. Beginning in the 1960s, government spending for spacecraft and warplanes provided the huge funding necessary for the early development of both hardware and software. These advances in turn helped push computer images into manufacturing and into medical applications such as plastic surgery. One spin-off from aerospace graphics has benefited hundreds of people with facial and cranial deformities caused by trauma, birth defects or tumors. In St. Louis, a team at Washington University Medical Center headed by plastic surgeon Jeffrey Marsh uses techniques developed by McDonnell Douglas for fighter-plane design to obtain a kind of preoperative blueprint: a structural model of the patient's skull.

The idea for this unusual adaptation originated with Michael Vannier, a government space engineer turned radiologist. With the help of engineers at McDonnell Douglas, Vannier adapted CAD software so that it depicts bones and flesh instead of the steel girders and aluminum skin of an F-15 fuselage. For raw material, the system relies on cross-section X-ray images obtained through the widely used method known as computer tomography, or CT scan. In CT scans, a patient's head is X-rayed from crown to neck at two-millimeter intervals; an adult's head could require 120 to 130 such X-rays, a child's less than half that number. The resulting images provide physicians with valuable information but are two-dimensional and difficult to read. The software Vannier developed for Jeffrey Marsh's team turns the CT-scan information into a three-dimensional computer image, which is then made to look more lifelike by a piece of software that drapes skin and muscle over the bare skull.

STRATEGIES FOR RECONSTRUCTION

Marsh can study the image on a computer screen to plan the surgical steps needed for reconstruction of the face or skull. He can peer inside the model or compare it with images of normal skulls. He can try out on the monitor various alternative surgical strategies and visualize the results without setting foot in the operating room. In addition, Marsh can test various procedures on three-dimensional physical models made from the same CT-scan information. "You can actually synthesize the surgery," he says of the computer-aided procedure.

While the St. Louis project makes use of graphics that provide both CAD and CAE, new medical technology developed in New York City takes the graphics process one step further by adding CAM, or computer-aided manufacturing. There, the Hospital for Special Surgery designs and produces custom-made hips, knees and other artificial joints with the help of its own CAD/CAM system. Before CAD/CAM, the process of designing and shaping an artificial joint typically required six weeks. First, a designer at the hospital studied conventional X-rays of the patient's diseased or damaged joint and hand-drew an artificial replacement. Next, a technician, working with lathes and milling machines, tried to shape a block of metal or plastic to replicate the drawing. Often the prosthesis failed to fit properly, and in the operating room the doctor had to perform more radical surgery on the patient in order to squeeze it in.

A computer does the job precisely—and in one third of the time and at one third of the cost. To design the prosthesis, a surgeon feeds into the computer data from CT scans and other X-rays of the afflicted joint. Variables that can affect the design, such as the patient's weight and level of activity, are also entered. The computer then selects an appropriate shape from 300 designs stored in its memory and displays it in three dimensions. "If the system doesn't have a model in its memory that works, it will generate another one that does," says the hospital's executive director, Donald Broas.

Working with a light pen on the screen, the surgeon and a design engineer fine-tune the image to ensure the closest possible fit with the patient's bone structure. The computer then punches out a tape containing the exact design coordinates for the artificial joint. The tape controls the lathes and milling machines that cut and shape the implant automatically.

The hospital envisions establishing a nationwide CAD/CAM network. Under this plan, orthopedic surgeons could design implants at terminals in hospitals almost anywhere in the United States and receive the finished product from New York a couple of weeks later in the mail.

Computer graphics are also finding widespread use in biomechanics, the branch of medical research that applies engineering principles to the study of human motion—in effect likening the body to an energy-efficient machine. Ali Seireg, the University of Wisconsin researcher who performs simulated surgery on the computer, is one of the leading authorities in the field. Seireg's work is based upon his remarkable computer model of human motion, which encompasses the body's entire muscular-skeletal system.

The model, which Seireg and his students developed over a period of more than a decade, contains some 1,200 equations relating to normal human movement, from walking to chewing gum. Some of these questions were determined statistically; others were based on experiments in which electronic sensors were attached to human subjects to record the forces that specific muscles exerted on bones as the subjects moved in front of a video camera.

In addition to being used in previewing surgical procedures, Seireg's model has also been applied in physical therapy. By analyzing a videotape of a patient's movements, the therapist can see how a given disability affects the entire body and determine which muscles need rehabilitation. In one case, after the computer was fed information on the patient's size, weight and injury, the model showed the patient the best way to use a cane to reduce stress on the injured hip.

COACHING BY COMPUTER
While Seireg's motion model helps people with disabilities, other researchers in biomechanics apply computer graphics to help the most able-bodied people of all—competitive athletes. By analyzing computer images of the athlete's performance, coaches can help enhance a golfer's swing, a tennis player's serve or a marathoner's stride.

The process begins with high-speed films of the athlete in action. From the individual frames of the film, the analyst and coach select the movements of specific parts of the body that illustrate the athlete's technique—the relative positions of the head, arms and shoulders of a golfer, for example. These images are converted into digital coordinates in the computer, which then generates a series of stick figures for careful study by the coach.

With some programs, minute analysis of technique is possible. These programs can display graphs showing velocity and acceleration, compare the performances of two different athletes or calculate such characteristics as the subject's center of gravity and the precise angle of elbow.

Such programs were credited with helping improve the performance of some athletes in the 1984 Olympic Games. Members of the United States' women's volleyball team, for example, not only studied their own performance but could study the competition's as well. Films of potential opponents were digitized and then analyzed for key weaknesses and strengths. Thus prepared, the Americans went on to win a silver medal for second place, the highest Olympic finish ever by a U.S. women's volleyball team.

In spite of such successes, researchers in biomechanics are quick to point out the limitations of comparing the human body with energy-efficient machines. "We tried to apply our model to one of this country's outstanding gymnasts," says Ali Seireg, "and found that this person was almost as energy-inefficient as he could be. But his movements were nonetheless beautiful. It just shows that we are not computer models, we're not perfect machines. We're flawed but beautiful humans."

Even as computer graphics systems are being used to study the mechanics of human motion, researchers in another field employ computer images to

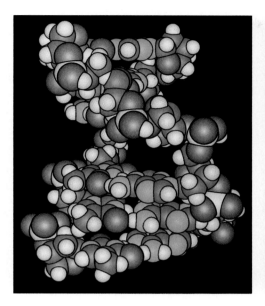
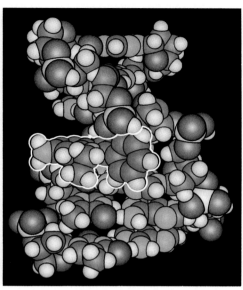

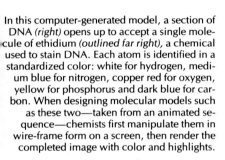
In this computer-generated model, a section of DNA *(right)* opens up to accept a single molecule of ethidium *(outlined far right)*, a chemical used to stain DNA. Each atom is identified in a standardized color: white for hydrogen, medium blue for nitrogen, copper red for oxygen, yellow for phosphorus and dark blue for carbon. When designing molecular models such as these two—taken from an animated sequence—chemists first manipulate them in wire-frame form on a screen, then render the completed image with color and highlights.

enter into submicroscopic realms and portray the beauty of a single molecule. In scores of biochemical research labs around the world, computer monitors can display multicolored models of molecules. The models are clusters of hundreds of little balls, each color-coded to represent a type of atom. To the researcher, who sometimes wears stereoscopic lenses to enhance the illusion of three-dimensional depth, the models seem to float in space. With a joystick cradled in each hand, the scientist can manipulate two models on the screen, maneuvering them toward each other. When they are in just the right juxtaposition, so that a protuberance on the surface of one fits neatly into a cavity on the other, the models come together and lock like a pair of spacecraft docking. This little drama simulates a key action in real biochemical behavior. Molecules of different substances couple by attaching to each other at specific receptor sites—an interaction that helps explain how a virus penetrates a cell.

Such a simulation would have been out of the question before the advent of sophisticated graphics programs. Although a method of electronic analysis known as X-ray crystallography can provide researchers with the relative positions of atoms in a molecule, scientists until recently could visualize the molecule only by constructing unwieldy physical models from wire and plastic balls. These Tinkertoy-like models of highly complex proteins, with their convoluted strands of amino acids, often filled an entire room.

Today, the atomic coordinates yielded by X-ray crystallography may be fed into powerful computer programs. In addition to displaying three-dimensional models in either wire-frame or solid modes, these programs can supply data on characteristics such as the molecule's solubility or the bonding between atoms. A biochemist can design a new molecule or change the structure of an existing one, all without dirtying a single test tube.

This kind of work has already brought about what one researcher describes

Explorations of the Fourth Dimensions

Just as biologists and chemists employ computer graphics to simulate the invisible behavior of molecules and atoms, researchers in other fields make use of computers to study abstract ideas that defy verbal description. A case in point is the so-called fourth dimension, a concept of abiding interest to physicists and mathematicians. In his Theory of Relativity, Albert Einstein considered time to be a fourth dimension. That is, an object is defined by its height, width and depth, with time as a fourth measure. Recently, some theoreticians have speculated about a fourth spatial dimension, no different in character from the other three.

Mathematicians can define hypothetical objects in higher dimensions with complex equations, but it is difficult for inhabitants of a three-dimensional world to visualize them. In theory, for example, a four-dimensional sphere moving through three-dimensional space might look like a point

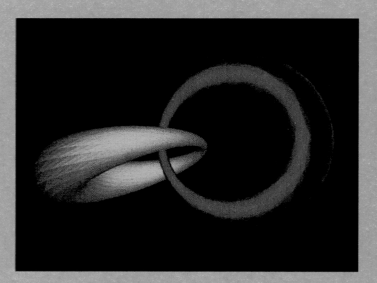
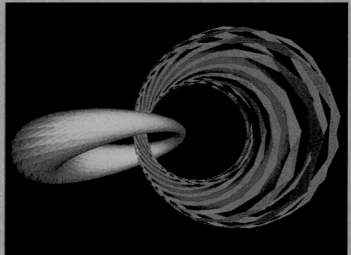
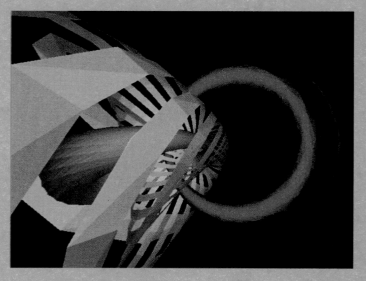
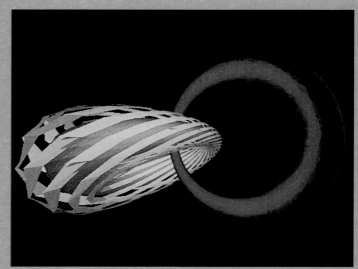

that suddenly appears from nowhere, becomes a tiny sphere that grows larger, then smaller—and then just as suddenly disappears. While this may be a reasonable representation, it does not give much useful information about the way such a sphere—called a hypersphere—looks in the fourth dimension itself.

A computer, however, has none of the usual human preconceptions; given the right numbers and a sophisticated program, it can easily illustrate four-dimensional analogues of three-dimensional objects. The images shown here, representing perspective views of objects on a hypersphere, were taken from a computer-animated film created by a Brown University team headed by mathematicians Thomas Banchoff and Huseyin Kocak. "What we do, essentially," Banchoff says, "is take a 3-D snapshot of a 4-D object, then walk around it and accumulate enough views to understand it."

Although such images seem to live on the edge of fantasy, scientists are putting the fourth dimension to practical use in graphing complex equations that have four variables. For example, by plotting salinity, temperature, living matter and the strength of the current at given points in the ocean, the U.S. Office of Naval Research hopes to improve the monitoring of acoustic signals traveling through water. Meanwhile, physicists are exploring the possible existence of systems that require not just four but as many as 11 dimensions to define them.

5

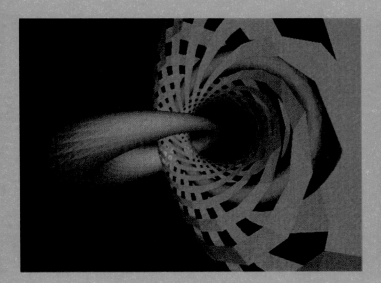

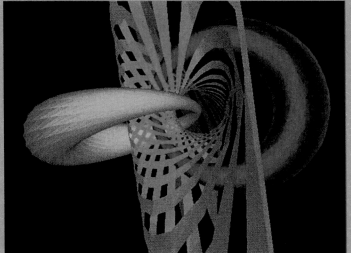

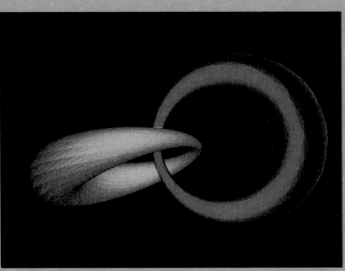

In a sequence of images from a computer-animated film, two interlinked toroidal, or doughnut-shaped, surfaces represent three-dimensional perspective projections of objects on a sphere in four-dimensional space. A third toroid, cut into bands to reveal its connection with the other two, appears to turn inside out as it moves from the magenta surface to envelop the green one.

as "a total revolution in chemistry." The impact is most evident in the design of vaccines and drugs. For example, in studies carried out by California's Research Institute at Scripps Clinic, in collaboration with the Lawrence Livermore National Laboratory, solid-modeling techniques were used to create a realistic view of the molecular structure of a virus that attacks tomato plants. From this image, biochemists identified the parts of the virus that could be imitated in the structure of a potential vaccine, which in turn would stimulate the host to produce antibodies.

Pharmaceutical firms consider molecular graphics indispensable in designing drugs and simulating their effects. Tests that used to require five weeks or more to single out the most promising compounds for intensive laboratory investigation can now be run on the computer in a matter of hours.

Other types of companies dependent upon chemical synthesis have turned to molecular graphics in their search for better designs for products ranging from herbicides and photographic films to soaps and sweeteners. One of the most advanced molecular-modeling systems in the world belongs to the industrial giant Du Pont, which by the mid-1980s had graphics terminals for anyone in its central research department who wanted one. Many Du Pont researchers even have terminals in their homes. David A. Pensak, chief of the company's molecular-modeling and artificial intelligence programs, plugs problems into his home terminal on autumn Sundays and works on them during commercial breaks in televised professional football games. Pensak is so enthusiastic that he ordered a specially tailored flight simulator to help other Du Pont researchers become similarly enthralled with molecular graphics. "Conceptually, landing a 747 on an airfield strip is no different from landing a molecule on an enzyme receptor site in the body," he says. "We want our people to feel like drug molecules, to be able to climb through molecules." The simulator is so popular, Pensak reports, that "people line up to use it."

A WORLD OF DYNAMIC DETAIL
It is in the simulation of flying, in fact, that computer graphics reach the highest level of realism and technical complexity. Though flight simulators help train civilian pilots, the most elaborate versions belong to the U.S. military. A pilot sits in a cockpit, which is an exact replica of the aircraft's, experiencing all the sights and sounds—even physical motions such as acceleration and air turbulence— of a particular mission.

On the cockpit windows in front of the pilot are projected a computer-generated, TV-like view of the world he would see on that mission. Virtually every detail is tailored for realism—the intensity of landing lights flickering in the distance or the smoke spiraling from the tank the pilot has just destroyed by launching make-believe rockets. Most important, the view is dynamic. As the pilot flies the craft with the joystick and other controls, the view changes in response to changes in the altitude, speed and position of the plane. The view changes also in response to the commands of the instructor, who, sitting at a control panel offstage, can introduce surprise elements such as an unexpected blanket of fog or an aircraft malfunction.

Such realism is made possible by software that draws from an enormous data base with millions of lines of picture information. By the mid-1980s, the world's largest visual data base, contained in General Electric's C-130 transport mission simulator, could reproduce views covering no fewer than 33,000 square nautical miles surrounding Little Rock Air Force Base in Arkansas.

Most data-base imagery is digitized from scale models or photographs of objects such as tanks and airplanes and from topological maps of the landscape that have been converted into a three-axis grid of coordinates containing contours of the terrain. But new programs also contain built-in generic terrain features such as forests and fields, which then can be embellished with roads, houses and other standard items.

Stored-up images must be generated and displayed at a rate of 30 to 60 frames a second in order to prevent flicker and preserve the illusion of real motion. Thus, a single frame in a real-time simulator has to be created on-line, that is, while the simulator is running, in less than $\frac{1}{60}$ of a second. By contrast, a similar frame for special effects in movies or television is computed off-line and may require hours of calculations.

The key to the astonishing speed of simulation graphics is hardware enhanced especially for image generation. This hardware consists of a series of processors, organized in what is known as "pipeline" architecture, which sort the data and render it into images. The pipelines operate in parallel, each of them generating a different segment of the view displayed on the cockpit windows.

This combination of the most advanced hardware and software contributes mightily to the staggering cost of military flight simulators. A new simulator for the Navy's AV8-B Harrier carried a price tag of $50 million, about one half of it accounted for by the visual system. But simulators are still cheaper to fly—to say

Night landings at airports with difficult approach patterns can challenge even experienced pilots, which is why novices practice first on a flight simulator. The ultimate in graphics speed and power, flight simulators use a realistic cockpit *(diagram, inset)* and special-purpose hardware and software to duplicate the piloting experience. Feedback from cockpit controls produces an ever-changing scene on the windows of the simulator, requiring the computer to calculate and display at least 30 new three-dimensional shaded images per second.

nothing of being infinitely safer—than actual airplanes. An hour in the simulator comes to about one tenth the expense of an hour in the real thing. And for the space shuttle astronauts, who spend more than 8,000 hours each in a simulator, flying an actual mission to train would be too risky and expensive.

The future of computer graphics will depend not only on the quality of programming but also on continuing progress in the development of hardware and other technology. Leaders in graphics research foresee new advantages from advances in microchip design: memory chips with ever-increasing capacity to store the minute detail necessary for solid-modeled images, and faster, more powerful processor chips—operating in parallel rather than sequentially—to generate the images in real time. They even envision replacing the computer screen with three-dimensional laser-generated holograms so realistic that the viewer can stroll through them.

As the expense of both hardware and software plummets, graphics are beginning to descend from the lofty realm of mainframes and minicomputers into the everyday domain of the home computer. Among the intriguing possibilities ahead: desktop simulators for learning to drive a car without ever leaving home, inexpensive workstations that would enable home-movie enthusiasts to generate their own animated special effects, and electronic home-repair manuals on which the viewer would simulate fixing the car before attempting it for real.

This anticipated democratization of computer graphics will depend in turn upon finding better ways to communicate with the machine. Graphic devices such as onscreen icons for microcomputers represent a vital step in that direction, making the computer more accessible to users who may be intimidated by unfamiliar keyboard commands. But visionaries are looking forward to computers so friendly that novices can operate them through a combination of spoken commands and ordinary gestures of the hand. "Put that there," the user might say while pointing toward an image on the screen. Electronic sensors strapped to the wrist would help the computer understand this cryptic command by communicating the hand's precise position in space. To Andries van Dam, Brown University's eminent authority on computer imagery, this scenario evokes an old dream of his drawn from the comic pages. "For me," he writes, "the ultimate ideal is expressed in the old comic strip 'Mandrake the Magician': Mandrake gestures hypnotically . . . and in the twinkling of an eye a new scene, a new sensory environment, is conjured up."

Graphic Visions in an Electronic Medium

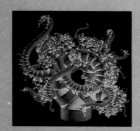

Advances in computer graphics have always had practical goals—to speed the design of energy-efficient automobiles, to manipulate the molecular structures of experimental drugs, to provide doctors with a clearer view of the human brain. But as graphic techniques have grown in sophistication, many programmers have been unable to resist using them to create art for its own sake. Working by day on powerful computers to produce images of molecules or asteroids, some scientists also spend their nights and weekends on the same machines, composing imaginative landscapes of the mind.

Joining them are traditionally trained artists who have learned to use the computer just as they would any other new medium. Representative samples of their creations appear on the following pages. Some artists, such as David Em *(pages 120-121)* or Mike Newman *(pages 118-119),* produce artwork for scientific organizations or computer manufacturers and thus have the advantage of easy access to high-powered machines and software. In these pioneering days of computer art, the software, memory and resolution available to the artist determine to a great extent the nature of the final image. Art produced with a ray-tracing program, for example, typically includes many shiny, reflective surfaces; if the piece is executed on a low-resolution monitor, however, those surfaces will have rough edges and a grainy quality.

Many computer artists use programmatic, noninteractive techniques: that is, they create pictures through mathematical procedures that will not yield a final image for hours or even days. These artists find the noninteractive process liberating in that it often produces serendipitous images. Other artists, however, value the computer as an artistic tool chiefly for its interactivity—its ability to change, erase, store and repeat pictures instantly.

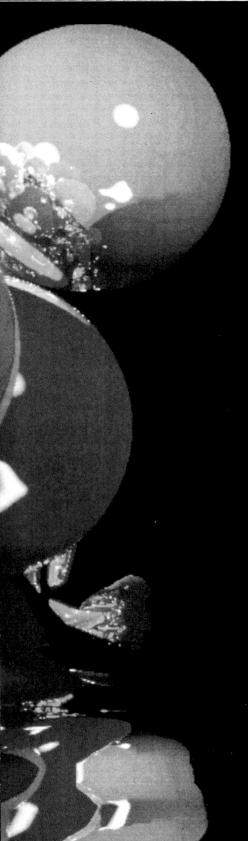

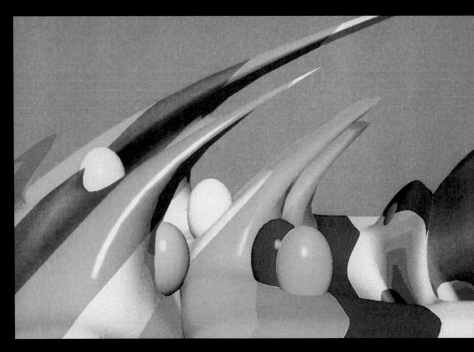

Images by Melvin Prueitt

Images by Mike Newman

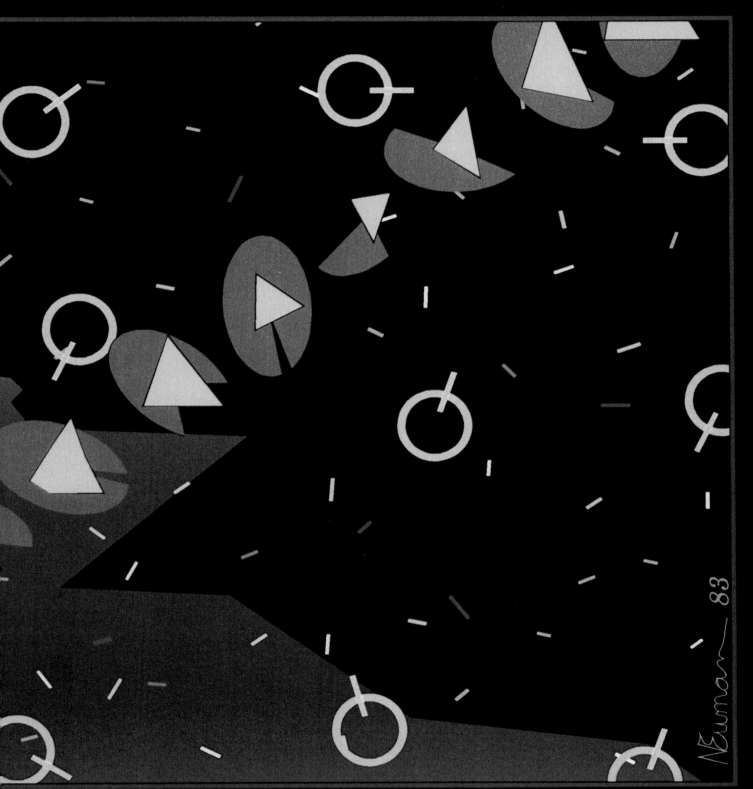

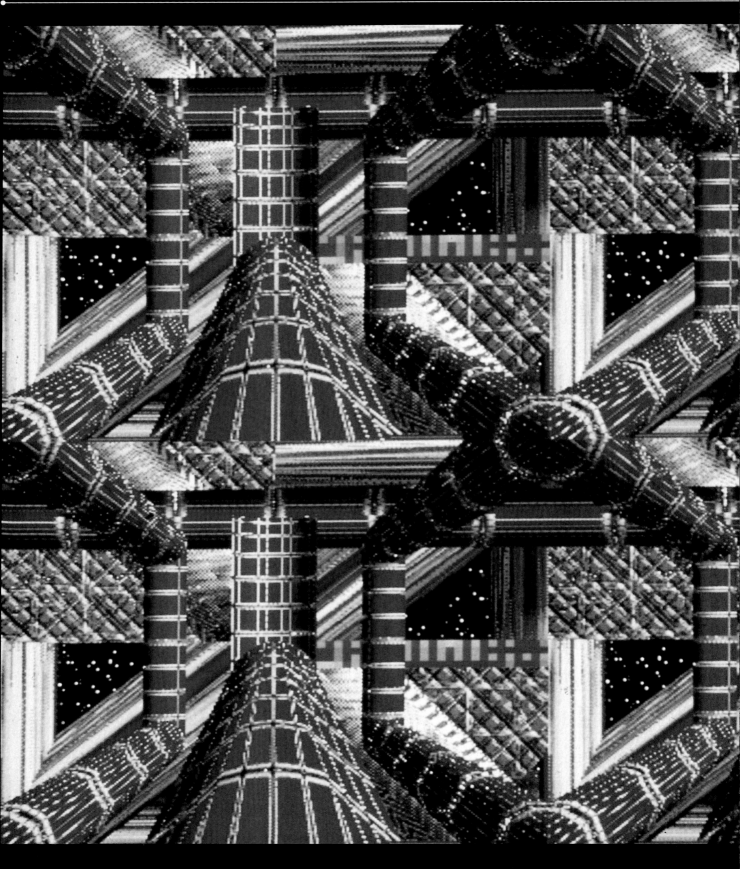

Images by David Em

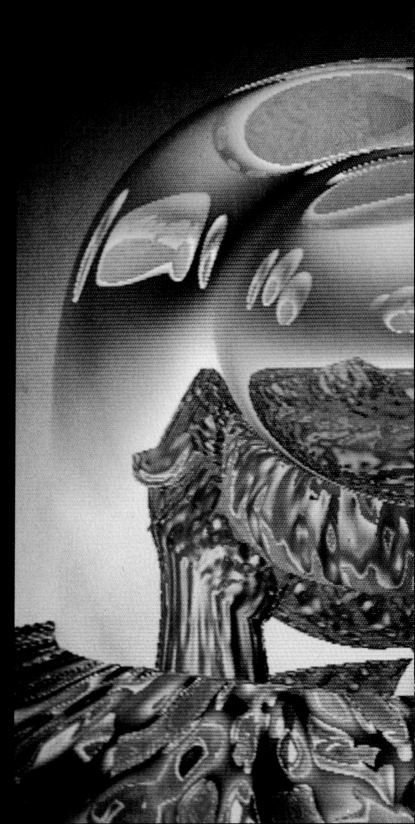

Images by Yoichiro Kawaguchi

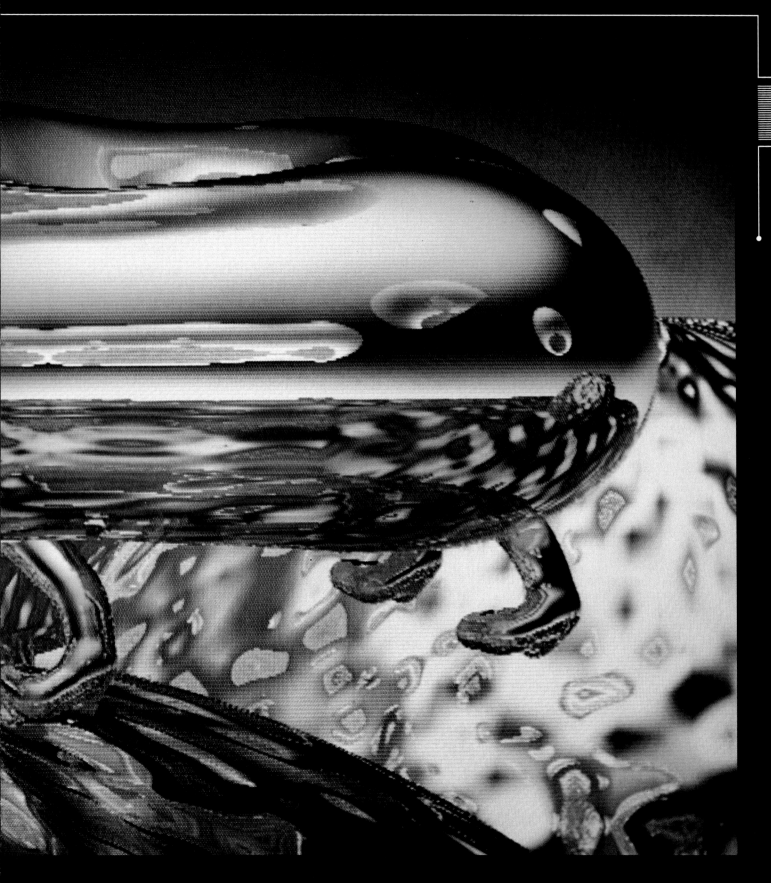

5

Bibliography

Books

Augarten, Stan, *Bit by Bit: An Illustrated History of Computers.* New York: Ticknor and Fields, 1984.

Bonifer, Michael, *The Art of TRON.* New York: Simon & Schuster, 1982.

Deken, Joseph, *Computer Images: State of the Art.* New York: Stewart, Tabori & Chang, 1983.

Gonzalez, Rafael C., and Paul Wintz, *Digital Image Processing.* Reading, Mass.: Addison-Wesley, 1977.

Greenberg, Donald, *The Computer Image: Applications of Computer Graphics.* Reading, Mass.: Addison-Wesley, 1982.

Jankel, Annabel, and Rocky Morton, *Creative Computer Graphics.* Cambridge: Cambridge University Press, 1984.

Mandelbrot, Benoit, *The Fractal Geometry of Nature.* San Francisco: W. H. Freeman, 1982.

Metropolis, N., J. Howlett and Gian-Carlo Rota, eds., *A History of Computing in the Twentieth Century.* New York: Academic Press, 1980.

Prueitt, Melvin L., *Art and the Computer.* New York: McGraw-Hill, 1984.

Redmond, Kent C., and Thomas M. Smith, *Project Whirlwind — The History of a Pioneer Computer.* Bedford, Mass.: Digital Press, 1980.

Rosenfeld, Azriel, and Avinash C. Kak, *Digital Picture Processing.* Vol. 1. New York: Academic Press, 1982.

Scott, Joan E., *Introduction to Interactive Computer Graphics.* New York: John Wiley & Sons, 1982.

Tatchell, Judy, and Les Howarth, *Understanding Computer Graphics.* Tulsa: EDC Publishing, 1983.

Periodicals

Alsop, Ronald, "Scientists Are Turning to Computers in Search for New Chemicals, Drugs." *The Wall Street Journal,* August 23, 1983.

Barrett, Charles N., "Preoperative Planning with Interactive Graphics." *Computer Graphics World,* March 1984.

Bernstein, Peter W., "Atari and the Video-Game Explosion." *Fortune,* July 27, 1981.

Bork, Robert H., Jr., "Of Potato Chips and Microchips." *Forbes,* January 30, 1984.

Bronson, Richard, "Computer Simulation: What It Is and How It's Done." *Byte,* March 1984.

Bylinsky, Gene, "A New Industrial Revolution Is on the Way." *Fortune,* October 5, 1981.

Campbell-Kelly, Martin, "Christopher Strachey, 1916-1975: A Biographical Note." *Annals of the History of Computing,* January 1985.

Chasen, Sylvan H., "Historical Highlights of Interactive Computer Graphics." *Mechanical Engineering,* November 1981.

Davis, Dwight B.:
"Chip-Based Graphics." *High Technology,* February 1985.
"Sports Biomechanics: Olympians' Competitive Edge." *High Technology,* July 1984.

Dumaine, Brian, "Designer Bones." *Fortune,* February 18, 1985.

Everett, Robert R., ed., "Sage (Semi-Automatic Ground Environment)." *Annals of the History of Computing,* October 1983.

Fichera, Richard, "24-Bit Color Graphics." *Computer Graphics World,* December 1983.

Fischer, Dennis K., *"The Last Starfighter:* A Computer Revolution in Special Effects." *Cinefantastique,* January 1985.

Gentry, Ric, *"The Last Starfighter." Millimeter,* June 1984.

Graff, Gordon, "Liquid Crystals." *High Technology,* May 1984.

Hacker, Randi, "Cartoons: How Computers Help Animate Them." *Computer Command,* November 1984.

Kindel, Stephen, "Designs for Living." *Forbes,* November 19, 1984.

Langridge, Robert, "Real-Time Color Graphics in Studies of Molecular Interactions." *Science,* February 13, 1981.

Lerner, Richard A., "Synthetic Vaccines." *Scientific American,* February 1983.

Love, Martin, "Better Bones." *Forbes,* November 21, 1983.

Machover, Carl, "Twenty-Five Years of Computer Graphics." *Computer Graphics World,* September 1983.

"Man-Machine Communication." *General Motors Engineering Journal,* Second Quarter 1965.

Marbach, William D., "The Factory of the Future." *Newsweek,* September 6, 1982.

Margolin, Bob, "New Flat Panel Displays." *Computers & Electronics,* February 1985.

Martin, Josh, "Fighting World War III with Quarters." *The Washington Monthly,* October 1984.

Mileaf, Harry, "Computers: The Evolution Is Over; The Revolution Is On." *Architectural Record,* June 1982.

Myers, Edith, "Cray Conquers H'Wood." *Datamation,* July 1, 1984.

Pollack, Andrew, "Math Technique Translates Chaos into Order." *The New York Times,* January 22, 1985.

Portugal, Franklin H., "Medical Imaging: The Technology of Body Art." *High Technology,* November/December 1982.

Prince, Suzan D., "In the Mind of Dr. Benoit Mandelbrot." *Computer Pictures,* May/June 1984.

Robley, Les Paul, "Digital Simulation for *The Last Starfighter." American Cinematographer,* November 1984.

Rosch, Winn L., "High Color Resolution Comes to Graphics." *Computers & Electronics,* April 1985.

Ruby, Daniel, "Biomechanics — How Computers Extend Athletic Performance to the Body's Far Limits." *Popular Science,* January 1982.

Schechter, Bruce, "A New Geometry of Nature." *Discover,* June 1984.

Schrage, Michael:
"Alan Kay's Magical Mystery Tour: The Search for the Ultimate Personal Computer." *Ambassador,* January 1984.
"Computer Animation Comes of Age in a Studio on 'Dopey Drive.' " *Smithsonian,* July 1982.

Shapiro, Neil, "How Computers Bring Cars to Life." *Popular Mechanics,* June 1982.

Shelton, Bill, "New Movie Magic: The Weird, Wild World of Special Effects." *Popular Mechanics,* December 1976.

Shuford, Richard S., "Two Flat-Display Technologies." *Byte,* March 1985.

Skow, John, "Games That People Play." *Time,* January 18, 1982.

Sorensen, Peter R., "Simulating Reality with Computer Graphics." *Byte,* March 1984.

Star, Jeffrey L., "Introduction to Image Processing." *Byte,* February 1985.

Tucker, Jonathan B., "Computer Graphics Achieves New Realism." *High Technology,* June 1984.

Van Dam, Andries:
"Computer Graphics Comes of Age: An Interview with Andries van Dam." *Communications of the ACM,* July 1984.
"Computer Software for Graphics." *Scientific American,* September 1984.

Vannier, Michael W., "Three-Dimensional Computer Graphics for Craniofacial Surgical Planning and Evaluation." *Computer Graphics,* July 1983.

Other Publications
"Computer Applications for Engineering and Manufacturing Company Vehicles." Dearborn, Mich.: Ford Motor Company.
"Computer Capability." Chicago: Skidmore, Owings & Merrill, 1980.
Machover, Carl, "Brief, Personal History of Computer Graphics."

IEEE Data Sheet, November 1978.
Raster Graphics Handbook. Covina, Calif.: Conrac Corporation, 1980.
Sutherland, Ivan E., *Sketchpad: A Man-Machine Graphical Communication System.* Technical Report No. 296. Massachusetts Institute of Technology, Lincoln Laboratory, January 1963.

Acknowledgments

The index for this book was prepared by Mel Ingber. The editors also wish to thank: **In the Federal Republic of Germany:** Stuttgart — Thomas Hartmann, Daimler-Benz. **In Great Britain:** Cambridge — Professor D. J. Wheeler, University of Cambridge; London — Lawson Noble. **In the United States:** California — Hollywood: Robert Abel, Robert Abel & Associates; La Mirada: Dr. Thurber Moffett; Los Angeles: David Em; John Whitney Jr., Digital Productions; Pasadena: Dr. James Blinn and Sylvie Rueff, Jet Propulsion Laboratory; San Rafael: Dr. Alvy Ray Smith, Lucasfilm; Delaware — Wilmington: Dr. David A. Pensak; District of Columbia — Seong K. Mun, Georgetown University Hospital; Georgia — Marietta: Dr. S. H. Chasen; Illinois — Chicago: Nicholas Weingarten, Skidmore, Owings & Merrill; Skokie: Dr. A. Hopfinger, Searle Research and Development; Maryland — College Park: Larry S. Davis, University of Maryland; Takoma Park: Mark Helgussen, Cybernetics; Michigan — Dearborn: Wayne C. Hamann, Ford Motor Company; Warren: Tom Roberts, BOC Advanced Design and Process Engineering; Minnesota — Burnsville: Mike Newman, DICOMED Corp.; Missouri — St. Louis: Dr. Jeffrey L. Marsh; Dr. Michael W. Vannier, Mallinckrodt Institute of Radiology; New Mexico — Los Alamos: Melvin Prueitt; New York — Binghamton: Peter Parsons, Singer; Elmsford: Carl Ludwig and Dr. Phillip Mittelman, Mathematical Applications Group, Inc.; New York: Mark Lindquist, Digital Effects; Bob Paxon, Hospital for Special Surgery; Judson Rosebush, Judson Rosebush, Inc.; Old Westbury: Dr. Frederic Parke and Lance Williams, New York Institute of Technology; Yorktown Heights: Richard Voss, IBM; North Carolina — Chapel Hill: Dr. Henry Fuchs, University of North Carolina; Ohio — Columbus: Dr. Thomas E. Linehan; Oregon — Wilsonville: Julie Grecco, Tektronix, Inc.; Pennsylvania — Pittsburgh: Dr. Ivan Sutherland; Rhode Island — Providence: Dr. Andries van Dam and Dr. Thomas Banchoff, Brown University; Utah — Salt Lake City: Dr. David C. Evans, Evans & Sutherland Computer Corporation; Virginia — Fairfax: Sheila Donoghue — National Computer Graphics Association; McLean: Philip Tashbar, Ramtek Corporation; Wisconsin — Madison: Dr. Ali Seireg, University of Wisconsin.

Picture Credits

The sources for the illustrations that appear in this book are listed below. Credits from left to right are separated by semicolons; from top to bottom by dashes.
Cover: David Margolis, photographer/created by Huseyin Kocak, Frederic Bisshopp, Thomas Banchoff and David Laidlaw/Brown University. 6, 7: Lucasfilm Computer Graphics Division. 9, 10: Art by Frederic F. Bigio from B-C Graphics. 11: Art generated by Isabel Nirenberg. 12: Mitre Corporation Archives. 15-29: Art by Kevin Hulsey. 30, 31: Wright-Patterson Air Force Base, Evans & Sutherland. 32: The M.I.T. Museum. 35: Art by Frederic F. Bigio from B-C Graphics. 36, 37: General Motors Corporation. 39: NASA/Goddard Space Flight Center. 40: Art by Matt McMullen. 41: Art by Aaron Bowles — NASA/Goddard Space Flight Center. 42, 43: NASA/Goddard Space Flight Center. 44: Art by Matt McMullen. 45: NOAA — NOAA/NESDIS. 46: Art by Matt McMullen — National Institutes of Health. 47: Art by Matt McMullen — Philips Medical Systems Inc. 48, 49: Dr. James F. Blinn/Computer Graphics Lab/JPL. 50: Garri Garripoli from Circuit Studios. 52: Art by Walter Hilmers Jr. from HJ Commercial Art. 53: Fil Hunter, photographer/digitized by Garri Garripoli from Circuit Studio. 55: Jules Bloomenthal/New York Institute of Technology(3) — art by Walter Hilmers Jr. from HJ Commercial Art(2). 56: © 1982 Gianfranco Gorgoni/Contact Press Images — © Sarah Putnam(2). 57: © Sarah Putnam. 58: © Melvin L. Prueitt, Motion Picture Group, Los Alamos National Laboratory. 59: Robert L. Cook/Cornell University. 61: Cranston/Csuri Productions, Columbus, Ohio. 62, 63: MAGI SynthaVision, Inc. 64: Copyright © 1982 by Paramount Pictures Corporation. All rights reserved — art by Aaron Bowles. 65: Alvy Ray Smith/Lucasfilm Computer Graphics Division. 66, 67: From *The Fractal Geometry of Nature* by Benoit B. Mandelbrot, San Francisco: published by W. H. Freeman © 1982; Richard F. Voss/IBM Research. 68, 69: Art by Aaron Bowles; Cranston/Csuri Productions, Columbus, Ohio. 70: Art by Aaron Bowles. 71: Ken Perlin and Gene Miller/MAGI SynthaVision, Inc. 72, 73: Mark Lindquist/Digital Effects. 74, 75: Lucasfilm Computer Graphics Division. 76: © 1982 Walt Disney Productions. 78, 79: Lance Williams/New York Institute of Technology. 81: © 1982 Walt Disney Productions. 82: MAGI SynthaVision, Inc. 84: Digital Scene Simulation (sm) by Digital Productions, Los Angeles, © Copyright 1984. All rights reserved; © 1984 Universal/Lorimar joint venture. All rights reserved. Courtesy of MCA Publishing Rights, a Division of MCA Inc. 85: Digital Scene Simulation (sm) by Digital Productions, Los Angeles, © Copyright 1984. All rights reserved. 86, 87: David Zeltzer, "Motor Control Techniques for Figure Animation" from *IEEE Computer Graphics and Applications,* © 1982 IEEE; David Zeltzer/M.I.T. 88: Susan Van Baerle and Doug Kingsbury, Computer Graphics Research Group, Ohio State University. 89: Lucasfilm Computer Graphics Division. 91: Skidmore, Owings & Merrill, developed by the Beacon Companies. 92, 93: Skidmore, Owings & Merrill. 94, 95: Skidmore, Owings & Merrill, developed by Paylor and Mathis. 96-99: Skidmore, Owings & Merrill, developed by the Beacon Companies. 100, 101: © 1985 Darcy Gerbarg/MAGI SynthaVision, Inc. 103: Daimler-Benz, Stuttgart. 105: Stanley L. Grotch/Lawrence Livermore National Laboratory. 106: Contour Medical Systems. 109: Nelson L. Max, © 1983 by the Regents of the University of California. 110, 111: David Margolis, photographer/created by Huseyin Kocak, Frederic Bisshopp, Thomas Banchoff and David Laidlaw/Brown University. 113: Evans & Sutherland, inset Rediffusion Simulation, Inc., overlay by Walter Hilmers Jr. from HJ Commercial Art. 115: Yoichiro Kawaguchi, Tokyo. 116, 117: © 1985 Melvin L. Prueitt Motion Picture Group/Los Alamos National Laboratory; © 1983 Melvin L. Prueitt Motion Picture Group/Los Alamos National Laboratory. 118, 119: Mike Newman/DICOMED Corporation. 120, 121: © David Em. 122, 123: Yoichiro Kawaguchi, Tokyo.

Index

Time-Life Books Inc.
is a wholly owned subsidiary of
TIME INCORPORATED

FOUNDER: Henry R. Luce 1898-1967

Editor-in-Chief: Henry Anatole Grunwald
President: J. Richard Munro
Chairman of the Board: Ralph P. Davidson
Corporate Editor: Jason McManus
Group Vice President, Books: Reginald K. Brack Jr.
Vice President, Books: George Artandi

TIME-LIFE BOOKS INC.

EDITOR: George Constable
Executive Editor: George Daniels
Editorial General Manager: Neal Goff
Director of Design: Louis Klein
Editorial Board: Dale M. Brown, Roberta Conlan,
Ellen Phillips, Gerry Schremp, Donia Ann Steele,
Rosalind Stubenberg, Kit van Tulleken,
Henry Woodhead
Director of Research: Phyllis K. Wise
Director of Photography: John Conrad Weiser

PRESIDENT: William J. Henry
Senior Vice President: Christopher T. Linen
Vice Presidents: Stephen L. Bair, Edward Brash,
Robert A. Ellis, John M. Fahey Jr., Juanita T. James,
James L. Mercer, Wilhelm R. Saake, Paul R. Stewart,
Leopoldo Toralballa

Editorial Operations
Copy Chief: Diane Ullius
Editorial Operations: Caroline A. Boubin (manager)
Production: Celia Beattie
Quality Control: James J. Cox (director)
Library: Louise D. Forstall

Correspondents: Elisabeth Kraemer-Singh (Bonn);
Margot Hapgood, Dorothy Bacon (London); Miriam
Hsia (New York); Maria Vincenza Aloisi, Josephine
du Brusle (Paris); Ann Natanson (Rome). Valuable
assistance was also provided by: Angelika Lemmer
(Bonn); Carolyn Chubet (New York).

Library of Congress Cataloguing in Publication Data

Main entry under title:
Computer images.
  (Understanding computers)
  Bibliography: p.
  Includes index
  1. Computer graphics.   I. Time-Life Books.   II. Series.
T385.C5932 1986   006.6   85-14050
ISBN 0-8094-5662-1
ISBN 0-8094-5663-X (lib. bdg.)

For information about any Time-Life book, please write:
Reader Information
541 North Fairbanks Court
Chicago, Illinois 60611

UNDERSTANDING COMPUTERS

SERIES DIRECTOR: Roberta Conlan

Editorial Staff for *Computer Images*
Designer: Robert K. Herndon
Associate Editors (pictures): Susan S. Blair,
Robert G. Mason
Series Administrator: Rita Thievon Mullin
Researchers: *Text Editors:*
Paula York-Soderlund   Lee Hassig
  (principal)   (principal)
Roxie France   Russell B. Adams Jr.
Denise Li   Donald Davison Cantlay
Tina S. McDowell   Peter Pocock
Writer: Patricia Daniels
Copy Coordinator: Anthony K. Pordes
Picture Coordinator: Renée DeSandies

Special Contributors: Ronald H. Bailey, Nikki Hardin,
Richard Immel, Donald D. Jackson, John I. Merritt,
Charles C. Smith (text); Enrico Caruso, Donn Fishbein,
Murray Loew, Marlin Perkins (research)

THE CONSULTANTS

LARRY ELIN is Vice President of Production at MAGI
SynthaVision, Inc., and is responsible for most of the animation produced at MAGI since 1973, including the
work on *TRON* covered in this book.

GARRI GARRIPOLI is President of Circuit Studios, Inc., a
computer graphics and video production company located in Washington, D.C. He is also Chairman of the Washington, D.C., Special Interest Group on Computer Graphics of the Association for Computing Machinery.

CARL MACHOVER is President of Machover Associates
Corporation in White Plains, N.Y., a consulting firm specializing in computer graphics. He is also an author, a
speaker and an adjunct professor of computer graphics at
Rensselaer Polytechnic Institute.

ISABEL LIDA NIRENBERG has dealt with a wide range
of computer applications, from the analysis of data col-
lected by the Pioneer space probes to the matching of
children and families for adoption agencies. She works
at the Computer Center at the State University of New
York at Albany.

OLIVER STRIMPEL is Associate Director and Curator at
the Computer Museum, Boston. Prior to joining the Computer Museum, he was Curator for Mathematics and
Computing at the Science Museum, London.

CHUCK WEGER has been active in computer graphics
for more than a decade. He is associated with Computer
Graphics Consultants, Washington, D.C., specializing in
user-interface design and graphics workstations.